THE COLLECTION OF STUFFED DOLLS
FROM A FANCY WORLD

BY KYOKO YONEYAMA

CONTENTS

★ Copyright © 1994 ONDORISHA PUBLISHERS., LTD. All rights reserved.
★ Published by ONDORISHA PUBLISHERS, LTD.,
  11-11 Nishigoken-cho, shinjuku-ku, Tokyo 162, Japan.
★ Sole Overseas Distributor : Japan Publications Trading Co., Ltd.
  P.O. Box 5030 Tokyo International, Tokyo, Japan.
★ Distributed
• in United States by Kodansha America, INC.
  114 Fifth Avenue, New York, NY 10011, U.S.A.
• in Canada by Fitzhenry & Whiteside LTD.
  195 Allstate Parkway, Markham, Ontario L3R 4T8, Canada.
• in British Isles & European Continent by Premier Book Marketing Ltd.,
  1 Gower Street, London WC1E 6HA, England.
• in Australia by Bookwise International
  54 Crittenden Road, Findon, South Australia 5023, Australia.
• in The Far East and Japan by Japan Publications Trading Co., Ltd.
  1-2-1, Sarugaku-cho, Chiyoda-ku, Tokyo 101, Japan.

10 9 8 7 6 5 4 3 2 1

ISBN 0-87040-933-6
Printed in Japan

FROM FAIRY TALES
Alice in Wonderland

INSTRUCTIONS ON PAGE 67

Karen in the Red Shoes

INSTRUCTIONS ON PAGE 72

Red-Riding Hood

MARY

CARRIE

he Big Woods

LAURA

JO

BETH

Women

MEG

AMY

INSTRUCTIONS ON PAGE 80

7

Monday's child is fair of face,
Tuesday's child is full of grace,
Wednesday's child is full of woe,
Thursday's child has far to go,
Friday's child is loving and giving,
Saturday's child works hard for a living,
But the child that is born on the Sabbath day
is bonny and blithe, and good and gay.

Monday's child

Tuesday's child

Wednesday's child

Thursday's child   Friday's child   Saturday's child   Sunday's child

The Sound of Music
MARIA

INSTRUCTIONS ON PAGE 87

My Fair Lady
ELIZA

INSTRUCTIONS ON PAGE 90

HUG-DOLLS

· *Rosalie* ·

INSTRUCTIONS ON PAGE 93

Ellen

INSTRUCTIONS ON PAGE 94

⓮

Mayu

⊖ INSTRUCTIONS ON PAGE 97
⊕ INSTRUCTIONS ON PAGE 98

Shigeru & Chiko

Midori & Oyuki

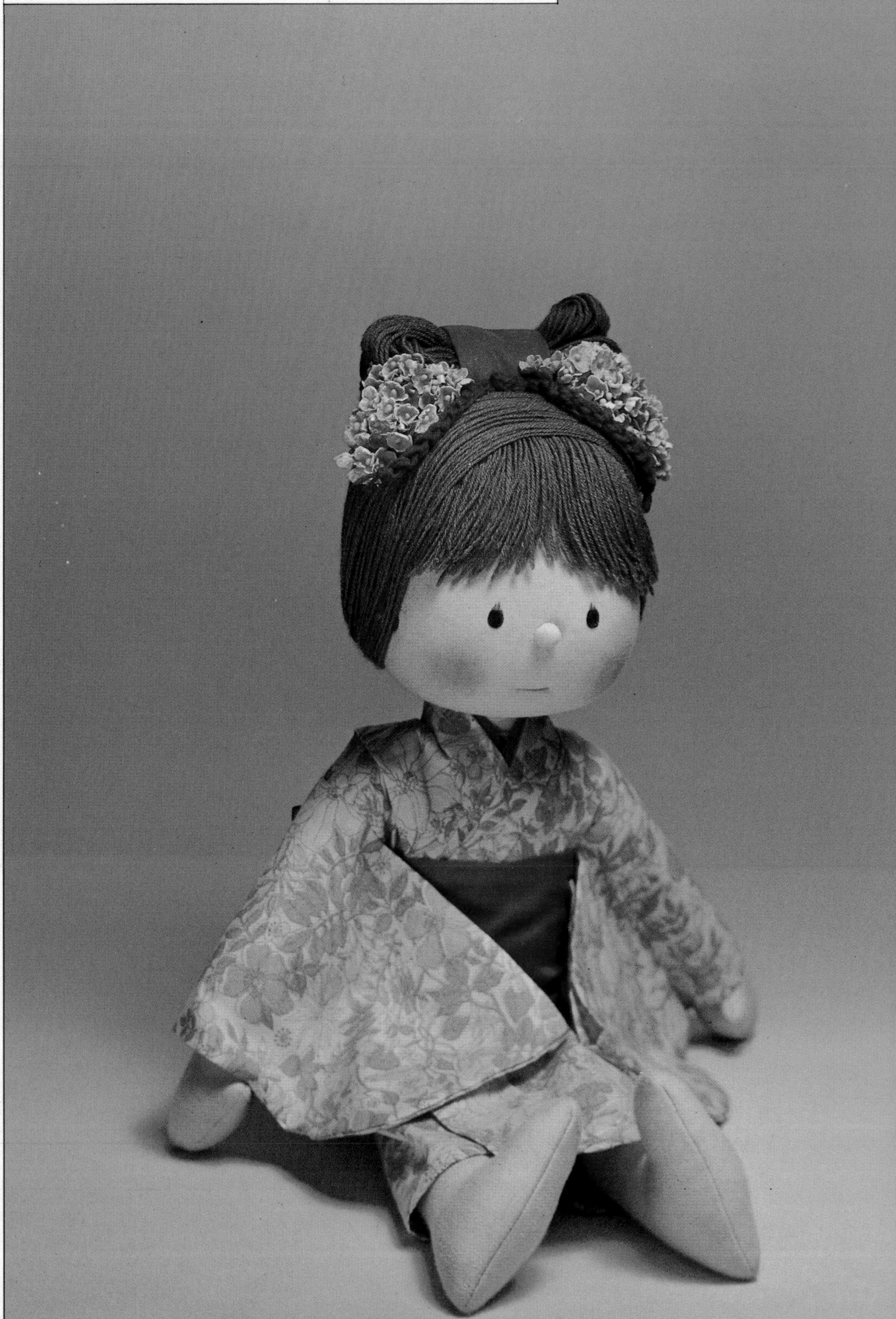

INSTRUCTIONS ON PAGE 106 ㉑

The Wood Elves

INSTRUCTIONS ON PAGE 109

Lost Angels

INSTRUCTIONS ON PAGE 110

㉓

INSTRUCTIONS ON PAGE 112

25

The Land of Unborn Babies

INSTRUCTIONS ON PAGE 114

Puck, Who Works for the King of Spirits

Pippi
Longstocking

INSTRUCTIONS ON PAGE 118

Willful Lotta

INSTRUCTIONS ON PAGE 119

The Gypsy
Fortune-Teller

INSTRUCTIONS ON PAGE 121

The Witch of
the New Moon

INSTRUCTIONS ON PAGE 124

INSTRUCTIONS ON PAGE 125

Miss Brenda, a Teacher from Tennessee

At Home on a Rainy Day

INSTRUCTIONS ON PAGE 130

Rapunzel
with Golden Hair

INSTRUCTIONS ON PAGE 131

Princess Elissa
in the Moon Light

Royal Princess
of the Stars

INSTRUCTIONS ON PAGE 136

INSTRUCTIONS ON PAGE 138

41

John & Barbara

INSTRUCTIONS ON PAGE 140

Mimi & Lulu & Popo

かぐや姫

Princess from the Land of Bamboo

INSTRUCTIONS ON PAGE 143

Glowing Sunset

MARIONETTES

Mitchi, the Hanging Doll

INSTRUCTIONS ON PAGE 146

Rommy & Doron

CLOTHING DOLL

Shirley

INSTRUCTIONS ON PAGE 152

LET'S MAKE "HIJI"

Hiji is an engaging hug-doll with a large oval head. Step-by-step directions for making her are shown on the following pages, and it's a good way for beginners to practice new skills.

You'll find that the secret of making a good doll is its foundation. Heads can be made larger or smaller, as you wish, but proper stuffing gives the doll a finished look. You can later vary their appearance by the shape and color of hair and clothing, and you'll find these projects are a good use for scraps in your sewing basket.

Welcome to the new pleasures of doll-making, then. You'll be creating thoughtful and personalized keepsakes in no time!

HIJI FINISHED SIZE: 37 cm tall

HOW TO MAKE "HIJI"

★ MATERIALS:

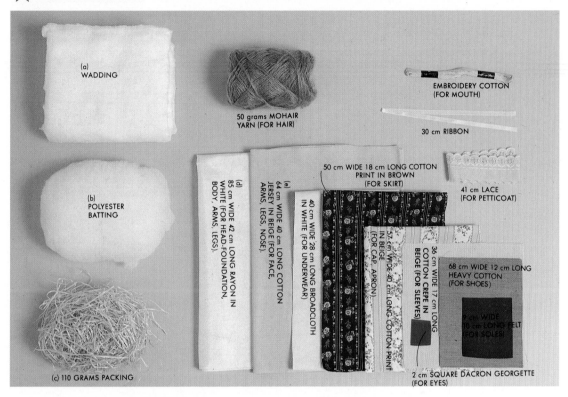

(a)
WADDING

50 grams MOHAIR
YARN (FOR HAIR)

EMBROIDERY COTTON
(FOR MOUTH)

30 cm RIBBON

(b)
POLYESTER
BATTING

(d) 85 cm WIDE 42 cm LONG RAYON IN WHITE (FOR HEAD-FOUNDATION, BODY, ARMS, LEGS).

(e) 64 cm WIDE 40 cm LONG COTTON JERSEY IN BEIGE (FOR FACE, ARMS, LEGS, NOSE).

40 cm WIDE 28 cm LONG COTTON BROADCLOTH IN WHITE (FOR UNDERWEAR)

50 cm WIDE 18 cm LONG COTTON PRINT IN BROWN (FOR SKIRT)

41 cm LACE
(FOR PETTICOAT)

57 cm WIDE 40 cm LONG COTTON PRINT IN BEIGE (FOR CAP, APRON).

36 cm WIDE 17 cm LONG COTTON CREPE IN BEIGE (FOR SLEEVES)

68 cm WIDE 12 cm LONG HEAVY COTTON (FOR SHOES)

9 cm WIDE 16 cm LONG FELT (FOR SOLES)

(c) 110 GRAMS PACKING

2 cm SQUARE DACRON GEORGETTE
(FOR EYES)

(a) to (e) are the materials needed to make the foundation; (a) to (c) are stuffing materials to form the foundation. Have extra amounts of stuffing material on hand. Other materials, such as yarn or cotton fabrics, can be selected from remnants you way have.

Assemble machine threads No. 50, 20, 8, and hand-sewing thread. When you make the foundation, use white thread with the long, heavy needle.

★ TOOLS:

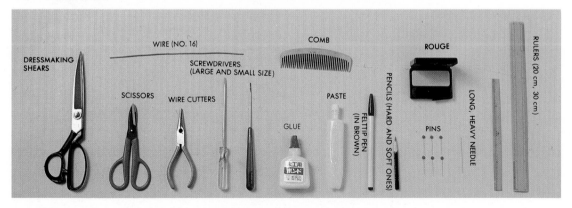

DRESSMAKING
SHEARS

WIRE (NO. 16)

SCREWDRIVERS
(LARGE AND SMALL SIZE)

COMB

ROUGE

RULERS (20 cm, 30 cm)

SCISSORS

WIRE CUTTERS

PASTE

GLUE

FELTTIP PEN
(IN BROWN)

PENCILS (HARD AND SOFT ONES)

PINS

LONG, HEAVY NEEDLE

1 TO MAKE PATTERNS:

Make cardboard patterns for accuracy. Copy each of the patterns below on tracing paper, and then transfer onto cardboard, making the outline with a hard pencil. Cut out the cardboard patterns carefully. Transfer the arrows, too, to show the grain of fabric for cutting.

PATTERNS (ACTUAL SIZE):

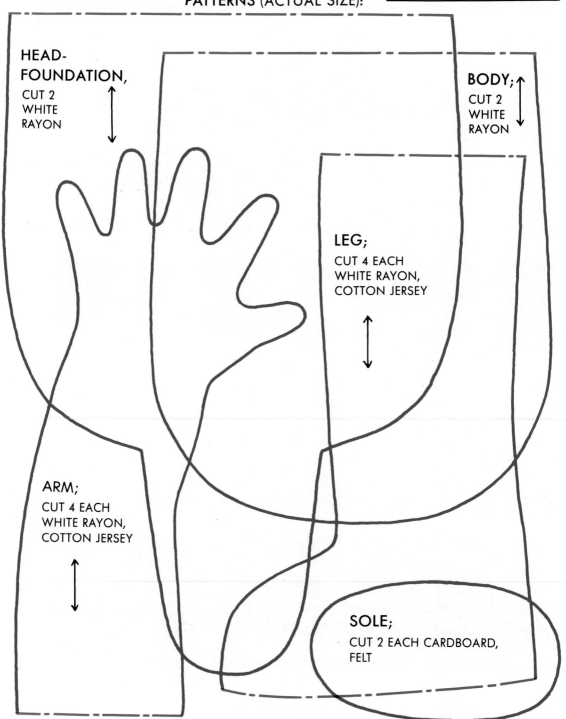

HEAD-FOUNDATION,
CUT 2
WHITE
RAYON

BODY;
CUT 2
WHITE
RAYON

LEG;
CUT 4 EACH
WHITE RAYON,
COTTON JERSEY

ARM;
CUT 4 EACH
WHITE RAYON,
COTTON JERSEY

SOLE;
CUT 2 EACH CARDBOARD,
FELT

2 TO SEW HEAD-FOUNDATION, BODY, ARMS & LEGS:

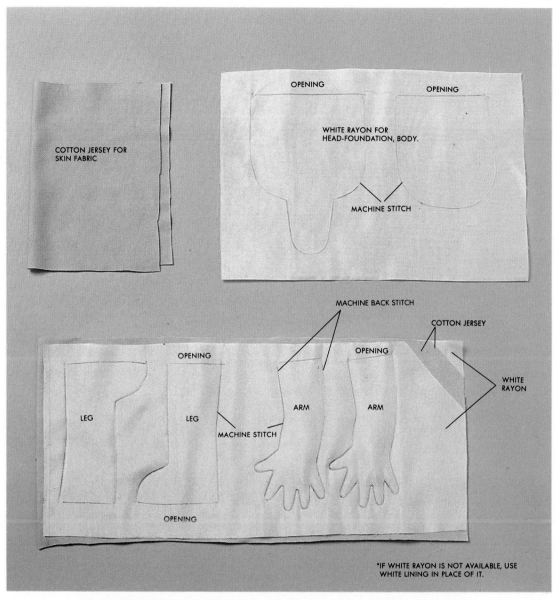

COTTON JERSEY FOR SKIN FABRIC

OPENING   OPENING

WHITE RAYON FOR HEAD-FOUNDATION, BODY.

MACHINE STITCH

MACHINE BACK STITCH

COTTON JERSEY

OPENING   OPENING

WHITE RAYON

LEG   LEG   ARM   ARM

MACHINE STITCH

OPENING

*IF WHITE RAYON IS NOT AVAILABLE, USE WHITE LINING IN PLACE OF IT.

Iron fabrics smooth. Trace the head-foundation onto white rayon, matching grain to arrows, and machine stitch.

Place the skin-colored jersey, right sides together, between 2 pieces of white rayon; then trace on the patterns for 2 arms and legs.

Machine stitch along traced lines, leaving an opening for stuffing.

Cut out the pieces, leaving the following seam allowances: 1.5 cm at openings of arms and legs, 0.6 cm around fingers, 0.2 cm on curved areas of fingers; and 1.5 cm around all the head-foundation areas of the body.

3 TO MAKE A HEAD-FOUNDATION & BODY:

Turn white rayon foundation pieces right-side out and stuff firmly with packing material, using a screw driver. If more packing is needed, adding it before completely stuffing in the first amount will give a smooth, firm finish.

① Finish the neck of the head-foundation as firm as a bar, stuffing to right above the opening line.

② Sew along opening, turn allowance to wrong side and draw stitches to close end firmly. Secure again, working a crossed stitch over it.

③ Stuff packing firmly into the body up to the opening. Lap the ends, matching opening lines together and pin it steady.

④ Secure firmly with 2 strands of No. 8 machine thread, making rough stitches.

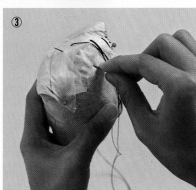
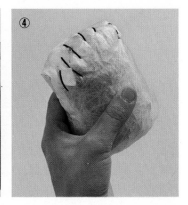

4 TO FORM THE BASE OF FACE:

Form the cotton wadding by tearing off the pieces needed with your hand. Head-foundation, jaw, and forehead are arranged as follows.

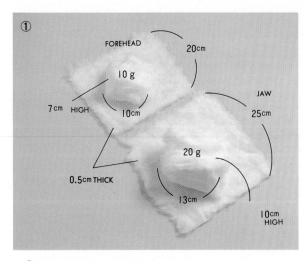

FOREHEAD
20cm
10 g
JAW
7cm HIGH
10cm
25cm
20 g
0.5cm THICK
13cm
10cm HIGH

① Make jaw first, and then forehead.

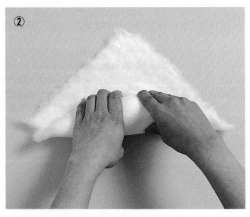

② Roll the piece up firmly, putting wadding piece for padding inside.

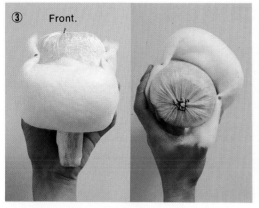

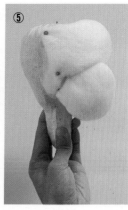

③ Attach jaw piece to the head-foundation with the jaw facing slightly downward, then make it steady with pins.

④ Sew on head-foundation with No. 8 machine thread doubled, drawing large stitches. Tear away surplus wadding on the sides.

⑤ Attach forehead. Pin the piece steady, drawing lower ends on both sides slightly over the jaw piece. Tear away the surplus wadding and tuck in all ends.

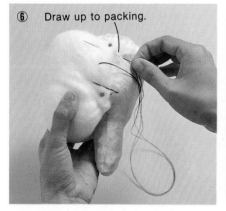

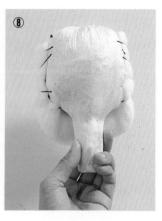

⑥ Stitch the ends at the side firmly to head-foundation.

⑦ Front

⑧ Back side

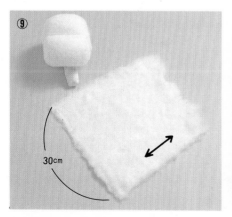

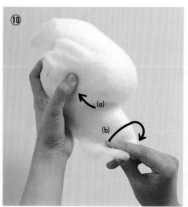

⑨ Spread wadding piece of 0.5 cm thickness. Lay on face at the bias.

⑩ Pull wadding upward, fitting to the shape of jaw (a). Wrap lower part round the neck as (b).

⑪ Smooth surface, fitting overlaid wadding carefully to the base. Tear away surplus at the back.

5 TO COVER THE BASE OF FACE WITH SKIN FABRIC:

Because of the elasticity of cotton jersey as a skin fabric, pin the ends of the stretched piece firmly to the base so the fabric does not become loose.

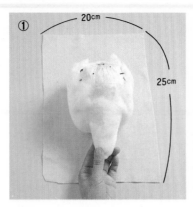

① Place face side down in the middle of skin fabric.

② Pin (a) to steady. Pull up the ends, both sides at a time, shoping the jaw. Pin (b) to the base so the fabric does not become loose.

③ Twist top corners, be careful not to make any folds on forehead; cross them on back and pin to hold steady (c).

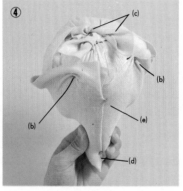

④ Fold back the surplus at back neck, and pin to hold steady (d) (e).

⑤ Stitch to the head-foundation with No. 8 machine thread doubled, pulling the fabric slightly upward.

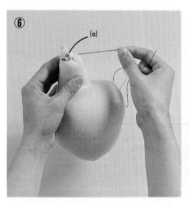

⑥ Secure (a) to the foundation, taking 3-4 stitches with single strand of No. 8 machine thread.

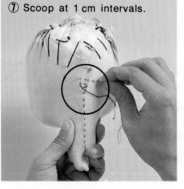

⑦ With No. 8 thread, work fine stitches taking care not to make the fabric loosen at center back.

⑧ Finished foundation.

6 TO ATTACH EYES, NOSE & MOUTH:

Experiment by placing eyes, nose, and mouth on face until you have the expression you want; then mark their position lightly on the face with a pencil.

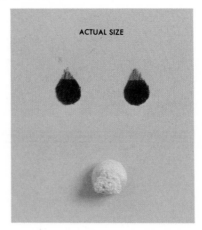

ACTUAL SIZE

TO MAKE A NOSE

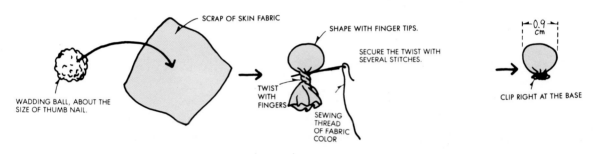

SCRAP OF SKIN FABRIC

WADDING BALL, ABOUT THE SIZE OF THUMB NAIL.

SHAPE WITH FINGER TIPS.

TWIST WITH FINGERS

SECURE THE TWIST WITH SEVERAL STITCHES.

SEWING THREAD OF FABRIC COLOR

0.9 cm

CLIP RIGHT AT THE BASE

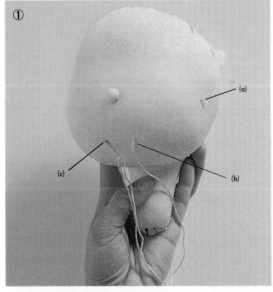

① Glue nose in position.
Use strands of cotton to make a mouth. Carry the needle through following (a) (b) (c) in turn, bring the needle out opposite (a), fasten off the thread, pulling sligthly.

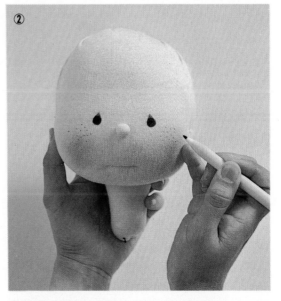

② Make eyes of dacron georgette. Pulling out upper crosswise threads to make eyelashes. Cut into shape and glue in place.
Apply rouge using wadding piece. Make freckles lightly with felttip pen. The ink might spread on the fabric, so try on another scrap first.

7 TO MAKE ARMS:

Make plump hands, stuffing wadding into fingers and polyester batting into arms.

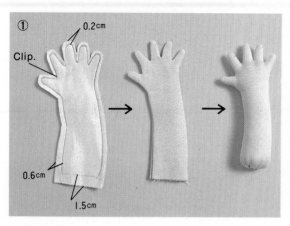

① Cut out arms with seam allowances, clip at the curve.

② Turn inside out using screw driver.

③ Turn fingers right side out one by one.

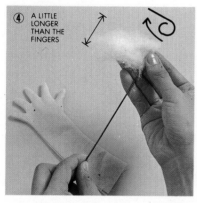

④ Wrap a piece of wadding round the No. 16 wire.

⑤ Insert into each finger and pull out the wire, leaving wadding piece inside.

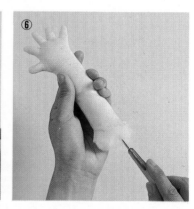

⑥ Stuff polyester batting into arm using screw driver. Put a little piece into palm side, making back side of the hand plump. Hand-stitch along opening, turning allowances inside, then fasten off.

8 TO MAKE LEGS:

Make legs, stuffing cotton wadding firmly.

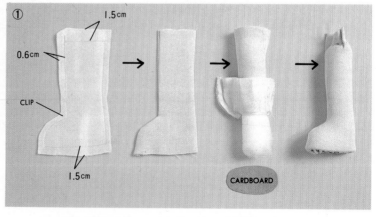

① Clip at the curve, then turn inside out.

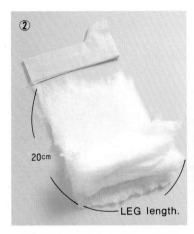

② Put wadding for padding on the stretched wadding piece.

20cm

LEG length.

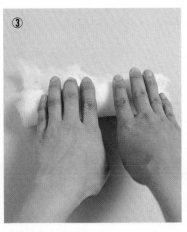

③ Roll together firmly into leg size.

④ Stuff rolled wadding into the top opening.

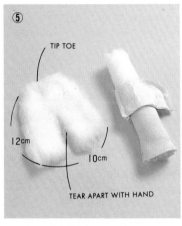

TIP TOE

12cm

10cm

TEAR APART WITH HAND

⑤ Make a piece of wadding for foot.

⑥ Put lower end of the leg between the tear, wrap with the next piece.

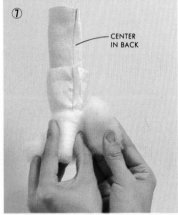

CENTER IN BACK

⑦ Lap surplus wadding at back, pull down the foot fabric above. Stitch top opening closed and fasten off.

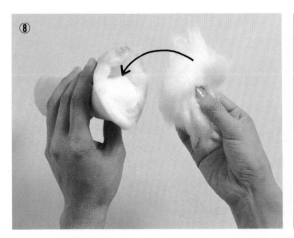

⑧ Stuff wadding up to the line of the sole.

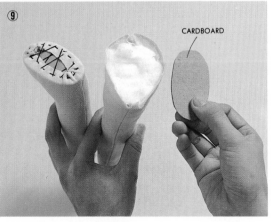

CARDBOARD

⑨ Insert the cardboard sole. Hand-stitch along the sole and draw the thread, overcasting a few times crosswise, then secure the end.

9 **TO PUT ON SHOES:**

Cut out the pieces of shoes from fabric, referring to page 62. Make with glue.

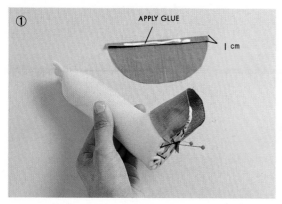

① Turn the edge of half-circle piece 1 cm to wrong side, apply glue on it. Pin it to foot, covering instep.

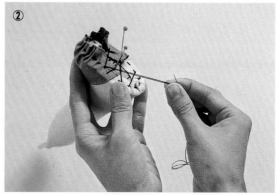

② Hand-stitch along the cut edge with No. 8 machine thread doubled, draw the thread overcasting a few times crosswise, secure the end.

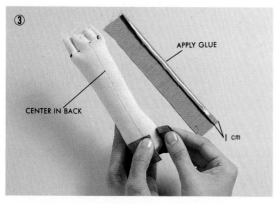

③ Turn 1 cm edge of oblong piece to wrong side, apply glue on it. Wrap the piece round the foot, turn the end at back to wrong side, pin to steady. Finish in fine slip-stitches with fabric color thread.

④ Hand-stitch along the edge with No. 8 machine thread doubled, overcasting crosswise, secue the end.

⑤ Pin felt sole to the base and sew on, working with fine slip-stitches.

⑥ Finished foot.

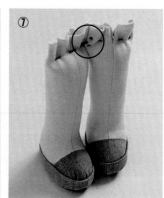

⑦ Put the finished legs together, join at the top taking a stitch to make their length the same.

1️⃣0️⃣ TO SEW EACH SECTION ON THE BODY:

Check each section to see if the work is correctly done, then sew on to the body.

① Sew legs firmly on body front with 2 strands of No. 8 machine thread.

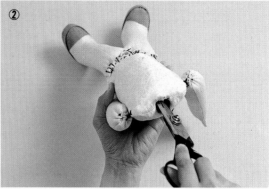

② Sew arms on body with a shank as button-sewing. Make a hole at the top of the body at right angles to the seam line; put scissors in and turn to enlarge to neck size.

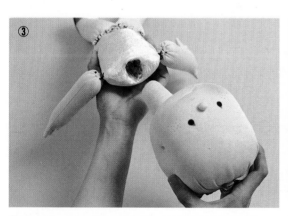

③ Insert the neck.

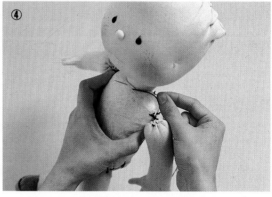

④ Stitch firmly (so the head doesn't totter) to the body, bringing the needle through the middle of the neck to the front with 2 strands of No. 8 machine thread.

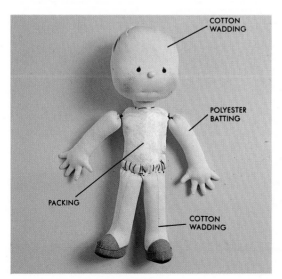

COTTON WADDING

POLYESTER BATTING

PACKING

COTTON WADDING

STUFFING MATERIALS:

Use three types of stuffing materials, packing, cotton wadding, and polyester batting to make the different part of the doll.

- Packing is strips of wooden shavings mainly used to form a head-foundation and body which finish has to be firm and solid.
- Cotton wadding is mainly used for the face, fingers, and legs which have to be finished softly and yet firmly. To get the sizes needed, tear off pieces roughly with hand instead of using scissors.
- Polyester batting is a convenient material, for it is springy without becoming bulky. Mainly used for the parts of amrs and legs where wanted to be formed softly.

11 TO SEW CLOTHES:

Doll's clothes are partly sewn beforehand, then each garment completed by sewing it to the body.

CUTTING GUIDE (INCLUDE SEAM ALLOWANCE)

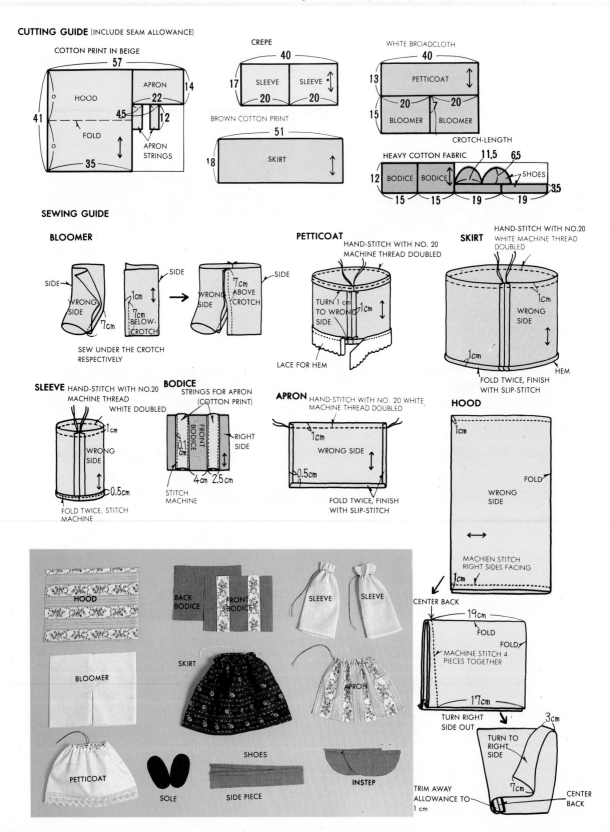

COTTON PRINT IN BEIGE
57
HOOD
APRON 14
22
41 4.5 12
FOLD
APRON STRINGS
35

CREPE
40
17 SLEEVE SLEEVE
20 20

BROWN COTTON PRINT
51
18 SKIRT

WHITE BROADCLOTH
40
13 PETTICOAT
20 7 20
15 BLOOMER BLOOMER
CROTCH-LENGTH

HEAVY COTTON FABRIC 11.5 6.5
12 BODICE BODICE SHOES 3.5
15 15 19 19

SEWING GUIDE

BLOOMER

SIDE
WRONG SIDE
7cm
SIDE
1cm
7cm BELOW-CROTCH
WRONG SIDE
7cm ABOVE CROTCH
SIDE
SEW UNDER THE CROTCH RESPECTIVELY

PETTICOAT

HAND-STITCH WITH NO. 20 MACHINE THREAD DOUBLED
TURN 1 cm TO WRONG SIDE
1cm
LACE FOR HEM

SKIRT

HAND-STITCH WITH NO.20 WHITE MACHINE THREAD DOUBLED
1cm
WRONG SIDE
1cm
HEM
FOLD TWICE, FINISH WITH SLIP-STITCH

SLEEVE

HAND-STITCH WITH NO.20 MACHINE THREAD WHITE DOUBLED
1cm
WRONG SIDE
0.5cm
FOLD TWICE, STITCH MACHINE

BODICE

STRINGS FOR APRON (COTTON PRINT)
FRONT BODICE
0.1 cm
RIGHT SIDE
4cm 2.5cm
STITCH MACHINE

APRON

HAND-STITCH WITH NO. 20 WHITE MACHINE THREAD DOUBLED
1cm
WRONG SIDE
0.5cm
FOLD TWICE, FINISH WITH SLIP-STITCH

HOOD

1cm
FOLD
WRONG SIDE
MACHIEN STITCH RIGHT SIDES FACING
1cm
CENTER BACK
19cm
FOLD
FOLD
MACHINE STITCH 4 PIECES TOGETHER
17cm
TURN RIGHT SIDE OUT
TURN TO RIGHT SIDE
3cm
7cm
CENTER BACK
TRIM AWAY ALLOWANCE TO 1 cm

HOOD
BLOOMER
PETTICOAT
BACK BODICE
FRONT BODICE
SKIRT
SOLE
SHOES
SIDE PIECE
SLEEVE
SLEEVE
APRON
INSTEP

12 TO SEW ON CLOTHES:

Sew on underwear first. Conceal cut ends or seam allowances with overlapped piece. Work fine stitches neatly where seen from outside.

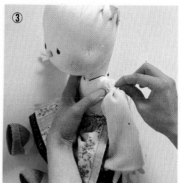

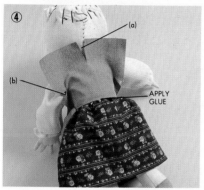

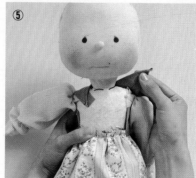

(a)

(b)

APPLY GLUE

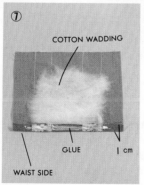

COTTON WADDING

GLUE   1 cm

WAIST SIDE

① Having drawn up lower ends of the bloomers, turn up waist section. Tuck at four places and secure. Put on petticoat, draw gather, and sew on body.

② Put skirt over petticoat, draw gather slightly above waist of petticoat, overlay apron and secure to the body.

③ Put sleeves on arms, stitch and gather at top, secure to shoulders. Gather sleeve-ends, stitching 1 cm from edge.

④ Turn lower edge of bodice back 1 cm to wrong side, apply glue. Put it over the allowance of the skirt, pin sides firmly. Clip at (a) & (b).

⑤ Turn the allowance at neck and arms to wrong side, pin the pieces from shoulders and sides to body front.

⑥ Stitch to the body with 2 strands of No. 8 machine thread.

⑦ Lay thin wadding piece on the wrong side of front bodice.

⑧ Put the piece on the body front turning allowances to wrong side, secure sides and shoulders working in fine slip-stitches with sewing thread.

⑨ Clothed doll.

13 TO SEW ON HAIR AND CAP:

Make a bundle of yarn 160 cm long (the same length as the skein of yarn clipped at the center). Put it on the head, smoothing with a coarse tooth comb.
Secure yarns following the arrows on the chart.

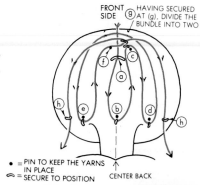

FRONT SIDE · HAVING SECURED AT (g), DIVIDE THE BUNDLE INTO TWO

• = PIN TO KEEP THE YARNS IN PLACE
⌢ = SECURE TO POSITION

CENTER BACK

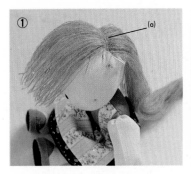

① Put front hair down on forehead, adjusting to the width of face. Steady with yarn carried across top (a) and slightly backward.

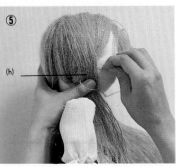

② Pin at the center back (b), bring yarn up to (c).

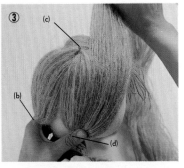

③ Pin at (c) & (d), place yarn as in (2). Pass the yarn to (e), putting widely along the outline of the face.

④ Having carried yarn across to point (g), secure at each point after (g) is secured to head.

⑤ Divide the remaining yarn in two, and bring down on both sides, secure at (h).

APPLY PASTE

⑥ Apply paste on forehead and at position of ears, attach yarn to the skin-fabric.

RIBBON

⑦ Trim front hair evenly. Braid yarn on both sides, secure ends with ribbon.

⑧ Place cap on head, secure above the front hair and at neck back with glue.

Completed Hiji.

CLARA

Shown on front cover.

A scalloped lace used for her dress, but you may use a fabric trimmed with lace instead.

YOU'LL NEED:
Head-Foundation, Body, Arms, Legs—90 cm by 21 cm white rayon. Face, Nose, Arms—45 cm by 25 cm beige cotton jersey. Legs—36 cm by 21 cm white jersey. Eyes—dacron georgette. Mouth—strands of embroidery thread. Hair—bouclé. Bloomer, Petticoat—80 cm by 18 cm white broadcloth, 40 cm of 3.5 cm lace, 50 cm of 3 cm lace. Dress, Cap—15 cm by 310 cm cotton lace fabric, 50 cm of 0.6 cm ribbon. Shoes—36 cm of 1.5 cm lace, 11 cm by 5 cm felt. Also—packing, cotton wadding, polyester batting.

FINISHED SIZE; Refer to diagram.
INSTRUCTIONS:
The basic method is the same as for Hiji, so refer to pages 50-64.
Make legs up to knee as for Hiji.
Make dress and cap with length of scalloped lace fabric.
Make hair by winding ringlets of yarn round a finger, secure each to head with machine thread, leaving proper space between. Secure to head all over without clipping the yarn following.

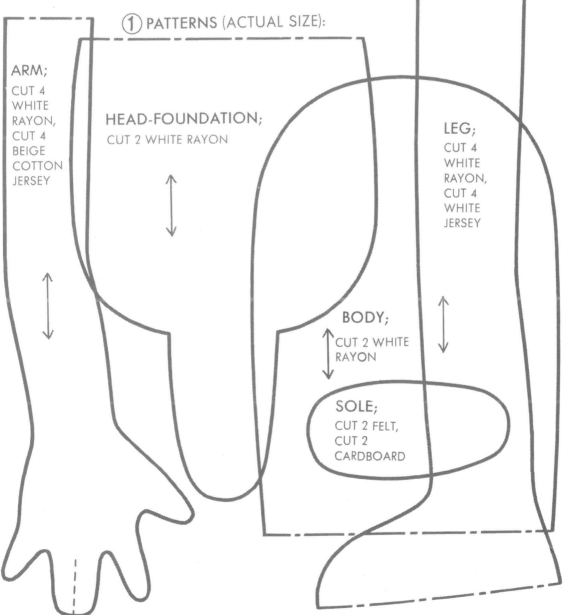

① PATTERNS (ACTUAL SIZE):

ARM;
CUT 4 WHITE RAYON, CUT 4 BEIGE COTTON JERSEY

HEAD-FOUNDATION;
CUT 2 WHITE RAYON

LEG;
CUT 4 WHITE RAYON, CUT 4 WHITE JERSEY

BODY;
CUT 2 WHITE RAYON

SOLE;
CUT 2 FELT, CUT 2 CARDBOARD

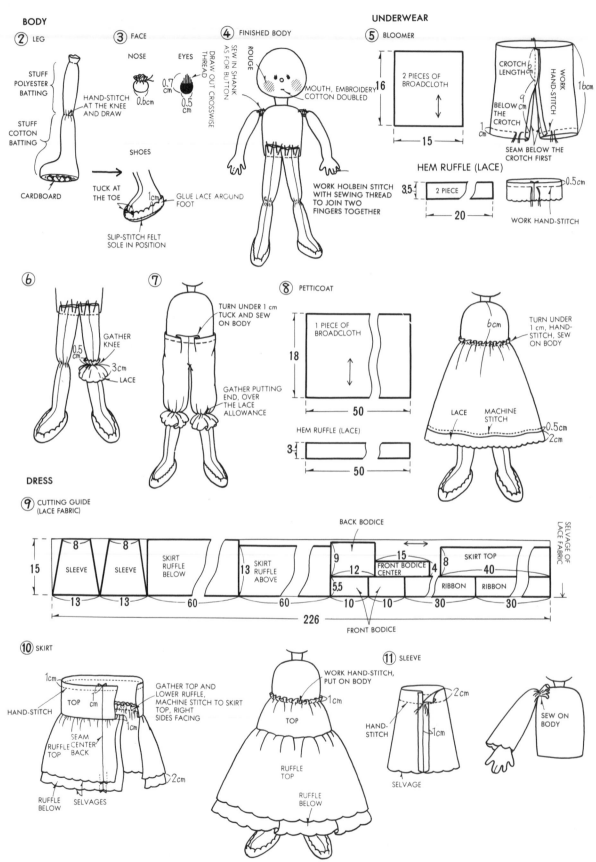

BODY

UNDERWEAR

② LEG

③ FACE

④ FINISHED BODY

⑤ BLOOMER

STUFF POLYESTER BATTING

HAND-STITCH AT THE KNEE AND DRAW

STUFF COTTON BATTING

CARDBOARD

NOSE

0.6cm

EYES

0.7 cm

0.5 cm

SEW IN SHANK AS FOR BUTTON

DRAW OUT CROSSWISE THREAD

SHOES

TUCK AT THE TOE

1cm

GLUE LACE AROUND FOOT

SLIP-STITCH FELT SOLE IN POSITION

ROUGE

MOUTH, EMBROIDERY COTTON DOUBLED

WORK HOLBEIN STITCH WITH SEWING THREAD TO JOIN TWO FINGERS TOGETHER

2 PIECES OF BROADCLOTH

16

15

CROTCH LENGTH cm

BELOW THE CROTCH

WORK HAND-STITCH

16cm

1 cm

SEAM BELOW THE CROTCH FIRST

HEM RUFFLE (LACE)

3.5

2 PIECE

20

0.5cm

WORK HAND-STITCH

⑥

GATHER KNEE

0.5 cm

3cm

LACE

⑦

TURN UNDER 1 cm TUCK AND SEW ON BODY

GATHER PUTTING END, OVER THE LACE ALLOWANCE

⑧ PETTICOAT

1 PIECE OF BROADCLOTH

18

50

HEM RUFFLE (LACE)

3

50

6cm

TURN UNDER 1 cm, HAND-STITCH, SEW ON BODY

LACE

MACHINE STITCH

0.5cm

2cm

DRESS

⑨ CUTTING GUIDE (LACE FABRIC)

BACK BODICE

15

8

SLEEVE

8

SLEEVE

SKIRT RUFFLE BELOW

13

SKIRT RUFFLE ABOVE

9

12

5.5

15

FRONT BODICE CENTER

4

8

SKIRT TOP

40

RIBBON

RIBBON

SELVAGE OF LACE FABRIC

13

13

60

60

10

10

30

30

226

FRONT BODICE

⑩ SKIRT

1cm

HAND-STITCH

TOP

1 cm

1cm

RUFFLE TOP

SEAM CENTER BACK

RUFFLE BELOW

SELVAGES

GATHER TOP AND LOWER RUFFLE, MACHINE STITCH TO SKIRT TOP, RIGHT SIDES FACING

2cm

WORK HAND-STITCH, PUT ON BODY

1cm

TOP

RUFFLE TOP

RUFFLE BELOW

⑪ SLEEVE

2cm

HAND-STITCH

1cm

SELVAGE

SEW ON BODY

66

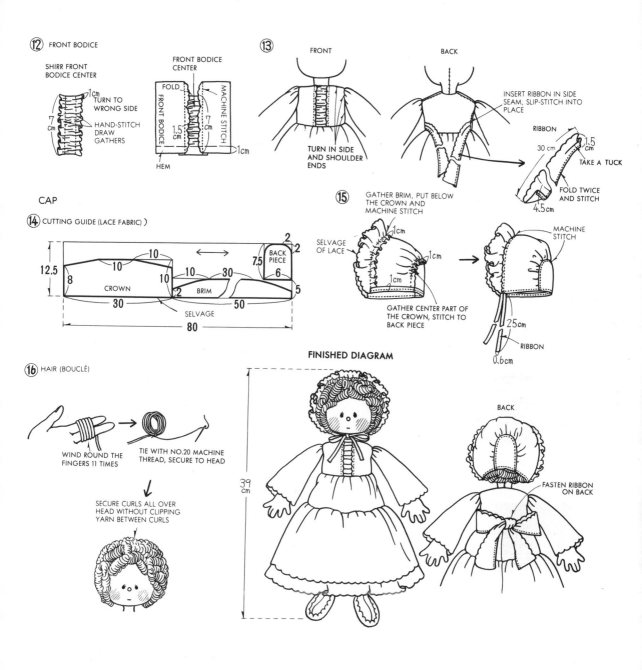

⑫ FRONT BODICE

SHIRR FRONT BODICE CENTER

1cm TURN TO WRONG SIDE

7 cm

HAND-STITCH DRAW GATHERS

FRONT BODICE CENTER

FOLD FRONT BODICE

MACHINE STITCH

1.5 cm

7 cm

1cm

HEM

⑬ FRONT

BACK

TURN IN SIDE AND SHOULDER ENDS

INSERT RIBBON IN SIDE SEAM, SLIP-STITCH INTO PLACE

RIBBON

30 cm

1.5 cm

TAKE A TUCK

4.5cm

FOLD TWICE AND STITCH

CAP

⑭ CUTTING GUIDE (LACE FABRIC)

12.5

8

10

10

10

10

30

2

BRIM

CROWN

30

SELVAGE

50

2

2

7.5

BACK PIECE

6

5

80

⑮ GATHER BRIM, PUT BELOW THE CROWN AND MACHINE STITCH

SELVAGE OF LACE

1cm

1cm

1cm

GATHER CENTER PART OF THE CROWN, STITCH TO BACK PIECE

MACHINE STITCH

25cm

RIBBON

0.6cm

⑯ HAIR (BOUCLÉ)

WIND ROUND THE FINGERS 11 TIMES

TIE WITH NO.20 MACHINE THREAD, SECURE TO HEAD

SECURE CURLS ALL OVER HEAD WITHOUT CLIPPING YARN BETWEEN CURLS

FINISHED DIAGRAM

39 cm

BACK

FASTEN RIBBON ON BACK

ALICE

Shown on page 1.

This hug-doll is easy to make. Packing should be stuffed firmly into the head. Mouth is drawn lightly with pencil and finished with embroidery.

YOU'LL NEED:
YOU'LL NEED:
Head-Foundation, Body, Arms, Legs—70 cm by 35 cm white rayon. Face, Nose, Arms, Legs—50 cm by 40 cm cotton jersey. Eyes—dacron georgette. Mouth—strands of embroidery thread. Hair—bouclé, 75 cm of 7 cm lace ribbon. Bloomer, Dress—90 cm by 40 cm cotton print, 56 cm of 3 cm lace, 270 cm of 2.5 cm lace. Also—packing, cotton wadding, polyester batting.
FINISHED SIZE; Refer to diagram.

INSTRUCTIONS:
The basic method is the same as for Hiji, so refer to pages 50-64.

Make legs stuffing polyester batting in same manner as for hands and finish openings the same way.

Having stitched decorative piece of front bodice and lace together, sew on body. Hand-stitch along the neck, gather and secure at back.

Sew on hair as for Red-Riding Hood on page 72, trim the ends evenly.

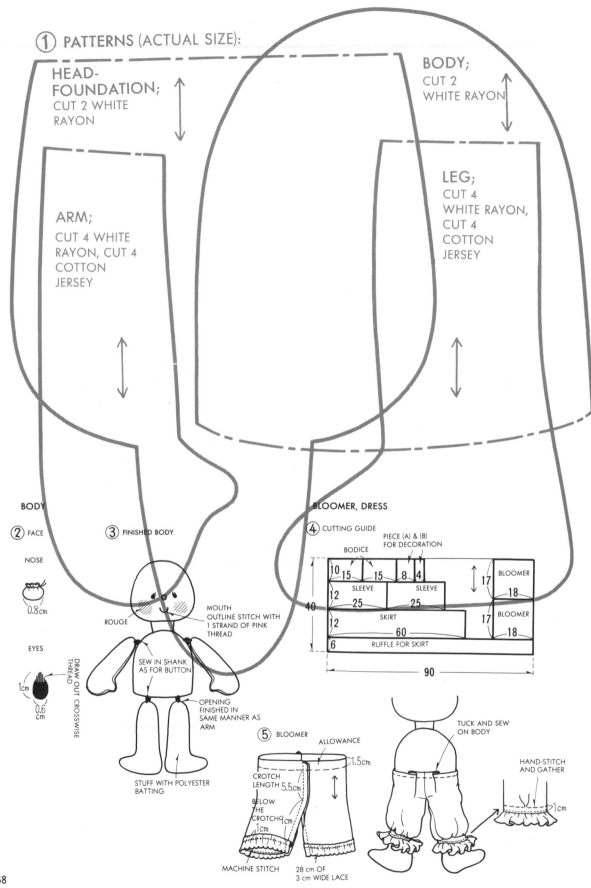

① PATTERNS (ACTUAL SIZE):

HEAD-FOUNDATION;
CUT 2 WHITE RAYON

BODY;
CUT 2 WHITE RAYON

ARM;
CUT 4 WHITE RAYON, CUT 4 COTTON JERSEY

LEG;
CUT 4 WHITE RAYON,
CUT 4 COTTON JERSEY

BODY

② FACE

NOSE

0.8 cm

ROUGE

EYES

1cm

0.6 cm

DRAW OUT CROSSWISE THREAD

③ FINISHED BODY

MOUTH OUTLINE STITCH WITH 1 STRAND OF PINK THREAD

SEW IN SHANK AS FOR BUTTON

OPENING FINISHED IN SAME MANNER AS ARM

STUFF WITH POLYESTER BATTING

BLOOMER, DRESS

④ CUTTING GUIDE

PIECE (A) & (B) FOR DECORATION

BODICE

10	15		15	8	4		BLOOMER 17
12	SLEEVE 25		SLEEVE 25				BLOOMER 18
40							
12	SKIRT 60						BLOOMER 17
6	RUFFLE FOR SKIRT						BLOOMER 18

90

⑤ BLOOMER

ALLOWANCE
1.5cm

CROTCH LENGTH 5.5cm

BELOW THE CROTCH 9cm

1cm

MACHINE STITCH

28 cm OF 3 cm WIDE LACE

TUCK AND SEW ON BODY

HAND-STITCH AND GATHER
1cm

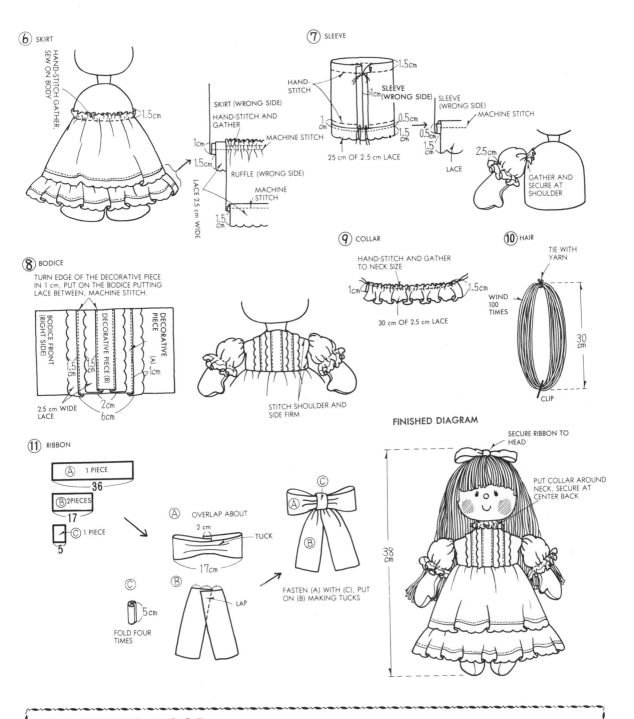

⑥ SKIRT

HAND-STITCH GATHER, SEW ON BODY

1.5cm

SKIRT (WRONG SIDE)
HAND-STITCH AND GATHER
MACHINE STITCH
1cm
1.5cm
RUFFLE (WRONG SIDE)
MACHINE STITCH
LACE 2.5 cm WIDE
1.5cm

⑦ SLEEVE

1.5cm
HAND-STITCH
1cm
SLEEVE (WRONG SIDE)
0.5cm
1cm
1.5cm
25 cm OF 2.5 cm LACE

SLEEVE (WRONG SIDE)
MACHINE STITCH
0.5cm
1.5cm
LACE

2.5cm
GATHER AND SECURE AT SHOULDER

⑧ BODICE

TURN EDGE OF THE DECORATIVE PIECE IN 1 cm, PUT ON THE BODICE PUTTING LACE BETWEEN, MACHINE STITCH.

BODICE FRONT (RIGHT SIDE)
DECORATIVE PIECE (B)
DECORATIVE PIECE (A)
1.5cm 1.5cm 1cm
2.5 cm WIDE LACE
2cm
6cm

STITCH SHOULDER AND SIDE FIRM

⑨ COLLAR

HAND-STITCH AND GATHER TO NECK SIZE
1cm 1.5cm
30 cm OF 2.5 cm LACE

⑩ HAIR

TIE WITH YARN
WIND 100 TIMES
30 cm
CLIP

⑪ RIBBON

Ⓐ 1 PIECE — 36
Ⓑ 2 PIECES — 17
Ⓒ 1 PIECE — 5

Ⓒ 5cm FOLD FOUR TIMES

Ⓐ OVERLAP ABOUT 2 cm TUCK 17cm

Ⓑ LAP

Ⓒ Ⓐ Ⓑ

FASTEN (A) WITH (C), PUT ON (B) MAKING TUCKS

FINISHED DIAGRAM

SECURE RIBBON TO HEAD
PUT COLLAR AROUND NECK, SECURE AT CENTER BACK
38 cm

RED-RIDING HOOD

Shown on page 3.

Select a colorful material for hood and dress. Try to finish them in different tones of color. (A checked fabric hood and apron might also be pretty.)

YOU'LL NEED:

Head-Foundation, Body, Arms, Legs—55 cm by 52cm white rayon. Face, Nose, Arms, Legs—65 cm by 52 cm cotton jersey. Eyes—dacron georgette. Mouth—strands of embroidery thread. Hair—sport-weight yarn, 40 cm of 0.3 cm ribbon. Bloomer, Petticoat—90 cm by 20 cm white broadcloth, 50 cm of 2 cm lace. Dress—82 cm by 37 cm seersucker. Vest—19 cm by 13 cm orange felt, ogrnge strands of embroidery thread. Apron—41 cm by 100 cm seersucker. Hood—22 cm by 45 cm red felt. Shoes—20 cm by 17 cm gray felt, Gray embroidery thread. Also—packing, cotton wadding, polyester batting.

FINISHED SIZE: Refer to diagram.

69

INSTRUCTIONS:
The basic method is the same as for Hiji, so refer to pages 50-64.
Make legs by stuffing with polyester batting as for arms.

Finish openings same way as arms. Sew shoes of felt.
Make hair separately, glue on head.

① **PATTERNS**
(ACTUAL SIZE):

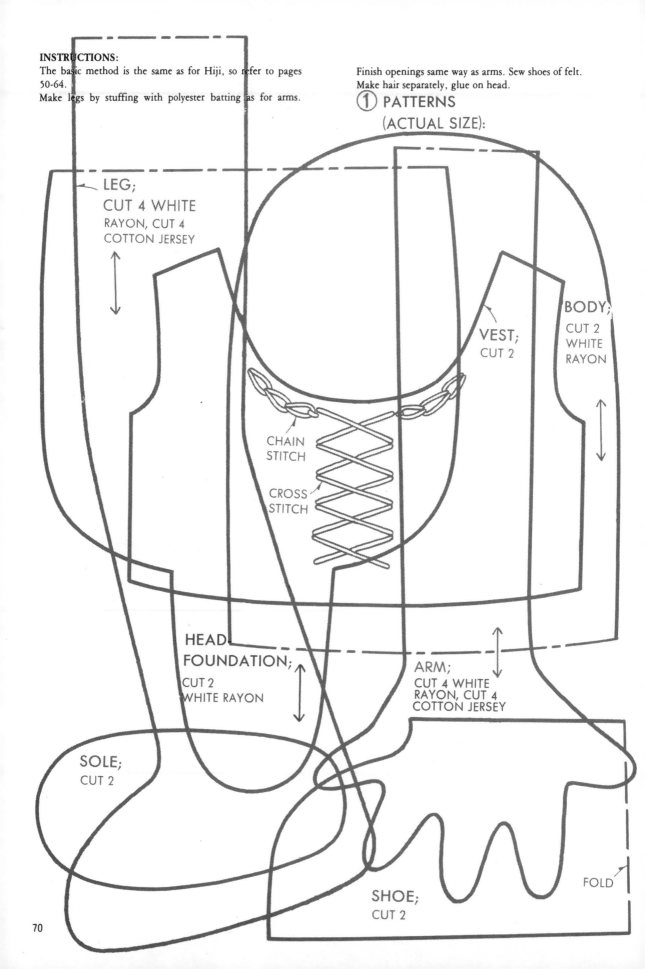

LEG;
CUT 4 WHITE
RAYON, CUT 4
COTTON JERSEY

VEST;
CUT 2

BODY;
CUT 2
WHITE
RAYON

CHAIN
STITCH

CROSS
STITCH

HEAD
FOUNDATION;
CUT 2
WHITE RAYON

ARM;
CUT 4 WHITE
RAYON, CUT 4
COTTON JERSEY

SOLE;
CUT 2

FOLD

SHOE;
CUT 2

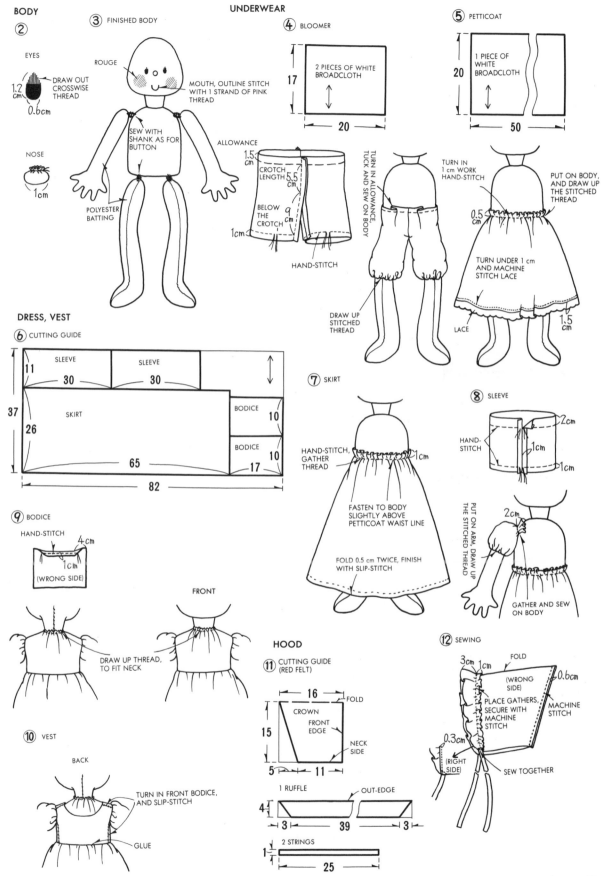

BODY

② EYES

DRAW OUT CROSSWISE THREAD

1.2 cm
0.6cm

NOSE

1cm

③ FINISHED BODY

ROUGE

MOUTH, OUTLINE STITCH WITH 1 STRAND OF PINK THREAD

SEW WITH SHANK AS FOR BUTTON

ALLOWANCE

POLYESTER BATTING

UNDERWEAR

④ BLOOMER

2 PIECES OF WHITE BROADCLOTH

17

20

1.5 cm

CROTCH LENGTH 5.5 cm

BELOW THE CROTCH

9 cm

1cm

HAND-STITCH

⑤ PETTICOAT

1 PIECE OF WHITE BROADCLOTH

20

50

TURN IN ALLOWANCE, TUCK AND SEW ON BODY

TURN IN 1 cm WORK HAND-STITCH

DRAW UP STITCHED THREAD

PUT ON BODY, AND DRAW UP THE STITCHED THREAD

0.5 cm

TURN UNDER 1 cm AND MACHINE STITCH LACE

LACE

1.5 cm

DRESS, VEST

⑥ CUTTING GUIDE

11

SLEEVE 30

SLEEVE 30

37

26

SKIRT

BODICE 10

BODICE 10

65

17

82

⑦ SKIRT

HAND-STITCH, GATHER THREAD

1cm

FASTEN TO BODY SLIGHTLY ABOVE PETTICOAT WAIST LINE

FOLD 0.5 cm TWICE, FINISH WITH SLIP-STITCH

⑧ SLEEVE

2cm

HAND-STITCH

1cm

1cm

PUT ON ARM, DRAW UP THE STITCHED THREAD

2cm

GATHER AND SEW ON BODY

⑨ BODICE

HAND-STITCH

4cm

1cm

(WRONG SIDE)

FRONT

DRAW UP THREAD, TO FIT NECK

⑩ VEST

BACK

TURN IN FRONT BODICE, AND SLIP-STITCH

GLUE

HOOD

⑪ CUTTING GUIDE (RED FELT)

16

FOLD

CROWN

FRONT EDGE

15

NECK SIDE

5

11

1 RUFFLE

OUT-EDGE

4

3

39

3

2 STRINGS

1

25

⑫ SEWING

3cm 1cm

FOLD

(WRONG SIDE)

0.6cm

PLACE GATHERS, SECURE WITH MACHINE STITCH

MACHINE STITCH

0.3cm

(RIGHT SIDE)

SEW TOGETHER

APRON

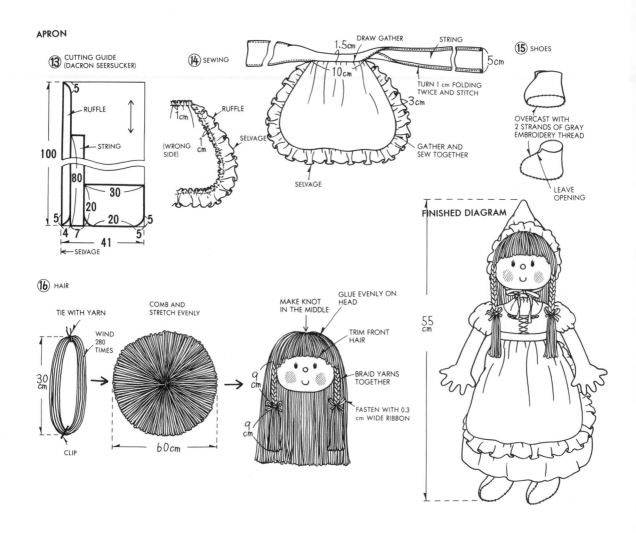

⑬ CUTTING GUIDE
(DACRON SEERSUCKER)

RUFFLE
STRING
100
80
30
20
20
5 5
5 4 7 41 5
SELVAGE

⑭ SEWING

1cm
(WRONG SIDE)
RUFFLE
SELVAGE
SELVAGE

DRAW GATHER   STRING
1.5cm
10cm
5cm
3cm
TURN 1 cm FOLDING TWICE AND STITCH
GATHER AND SEW TOGETHER

⑮ SHOES

OVERCAST WITH 2 STRANDS OF GRAY EMBROIDERY THREAD

LEAVE OPENING

⑯ HAIR

TIE WITH YARN
WIND 280 TIMES
30 cm
CLIP

COMB AND STRETCH EVENLY
60cm

MAKE KNOT IN THE MIDDLE
GLUE EVENLY ON HEAD
TRIM FRONT HAIR
9 cm
9 cm
BRAID YARNS TOGETHER
FASTEN WITH 0.3 cm WIDE RIBBON

FINISHED DIAGRAM
55 cm

KAREN

Shown on page 2.

The hat on her head is ready-made. You may crochet one of raffia, adjusting it to her head shape (refer to page 156). Felt way also be used for shoes.

YOU'LL NEED:
Head-Foundation, Body, Arms, Legs—90 cm by 60 cm white rayon. Face, Nose, Arms, Chest—65 cm by 30 cm cotton jersey. Legs—22 cm by 37 cm bleached cotton. Eyes—dacron georgette. Mouth—strands of embroidery thread. Hair-mohair yarn. Bloomer, Petticoat—80 cm by 51 cm white dacron georgette, 145 cm of 5.5 cm lace. Dress—90 cm by 240 cm nylon lace, 24 cm by 21 cm bleached cotton, 100 cm of 0.7 cm satin ribbon. Shoes—21 cm by 10 cm red suede. Also—packing, cotton wadding, polyester batting, hat.

FINISHED SIZE: Refer to diagram.
INSTRUCTIONS:
The basic method is the same as for Hiji, so refer to pages 50-64.
Finish the openings of legs as for arms. Put bodice on the body, laying bleached cotton underneath. Sew on sleeves and skirt with the fabric folded in half.
Put on skirt with seam lines on center back, sides in front.
Attach hair as shown above, trimming front hair evenly.

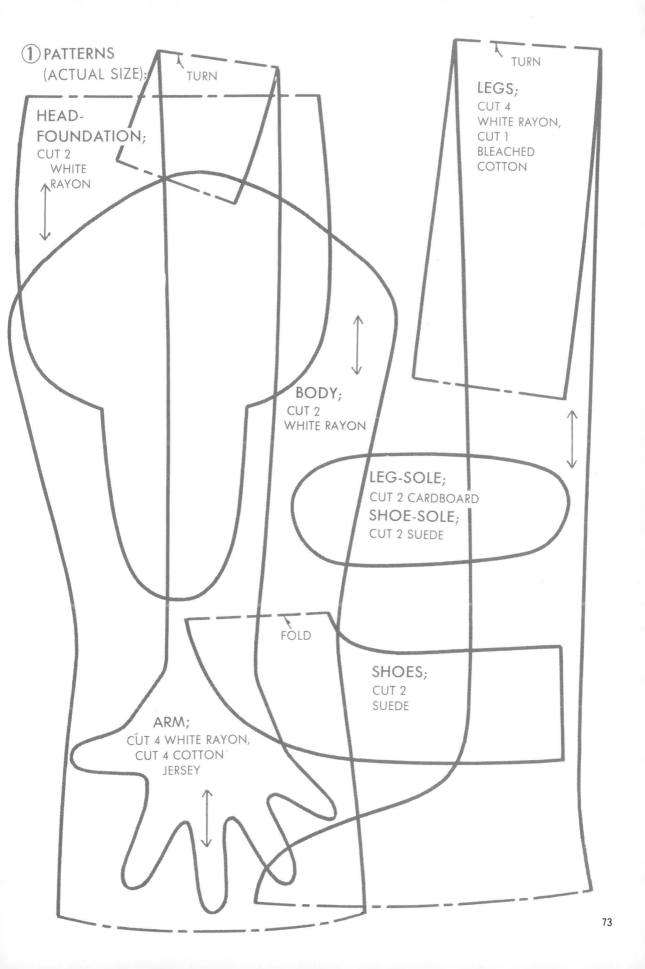

① PATTERNS
(ACTUAL SIZE):

TURN

HEAD-
FOUNDATION;
CUT 2
WHITE
RAYON

TURN

LEGS;
CUT 4
WHITE RAYON,
CUT 1
BLEACHED
COTTON

BODY;
CUT 2
WHITE RAYON

LEG-SOLE;
CUT 2 CARDBOARD
SHOE-SOLE;
CUT 2 SUEDE

FOLD

SHOES;
CUT 2
SUEDE

ARM;
CUT 4 WHITE RAYON,
CUT 4 COTTON
JERSEY

73

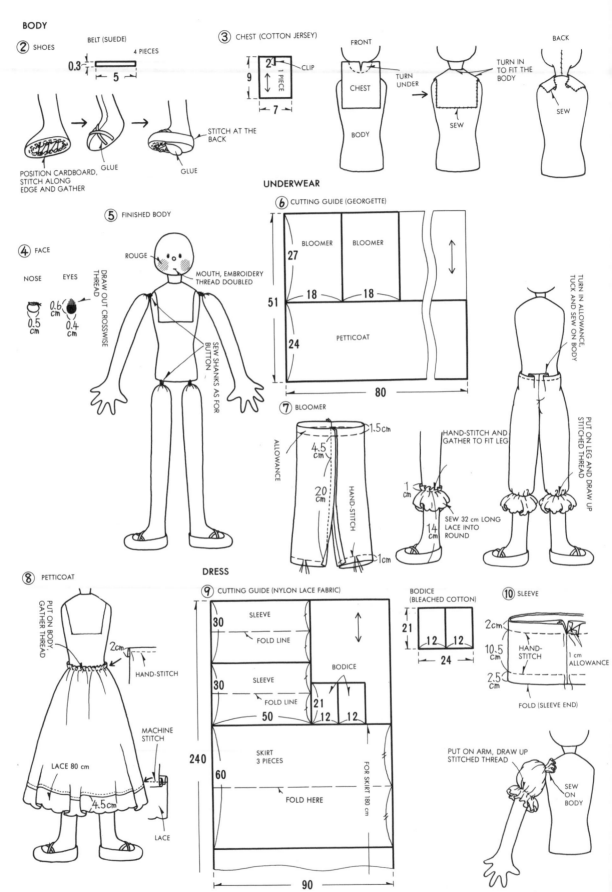

BODY

② SHOES

BELT (SUEDE)
4 PIECES
0.3
5

POSITION CARDBOARD, STITCH ALONG EDGE AND GATHER

GLUE

GLUE

STITCH AT THE BACK

④ FACE

NOSE
0.5 cm

EYES
0.6 cm
0.4 cm

DRAW OUT CROSSWISE THREAD

⑤ FINISHED BODY

ROUGE

MOUTH, EMBROIDERY THREAD DOUBLED

SEW SHANKS AS FOR BUTTON

③ CHEST (COTTON JERSEY)

21
9
7
1 PIECE
CLIP

FRONT
CHEST
BODY
TURN UNDER

TURN IN TO FIT THE BODY
SEW

BACK
SEW

UNDERWEAR

⑥ CUTTING GUIDE (GEORGETTE)

BLOOMER
BLOOMER
27
18
18
51
24
PETTICOAT
80

TURN IN ALLOWANCE, TUCK AND SEW ON BODY

PUT ON LEG AND DRAW UP STITCHED THREAD

⑦ BLOOMER

ALLOWANCE
1.5 cm
4.5 cm
20 cm
HAND-STITCH
1 cm

HAND-STITCH AND GATHER TO FIT LEG

1 cm
14 cm

SEW 32 cm LONG LACE INTO ROUND

DRESS

⑧ PETTICOAT

PUT ON BODY, GATHER THREAD

2 cm
HAND-STITCH

MACHINE STITCH

LACE 80 cm

4.5 cm

LACE

⑨ CUTTING GUIDE (NYLON LACE FABRIC)

30
SLEEVE
FOLD LINE

30
SLEEVE
FOLD LINE

50

BODICE

21
12
12

240
60
SKIRT
3 PIECES

FOLD HERE

FOR SKIRT 180 cm

90

BODICE (BLEACHED COTTON)

21
12
12
24

⑩ SLEEVE

2 cm
10.5 cm
HAND-STITCH
1 cm ALLOWANCE
2.5 cm
FOLD (SLEEVE END)

PUT ON ARM, DRAW UP STITCHED THREAD

SEW ON BODY

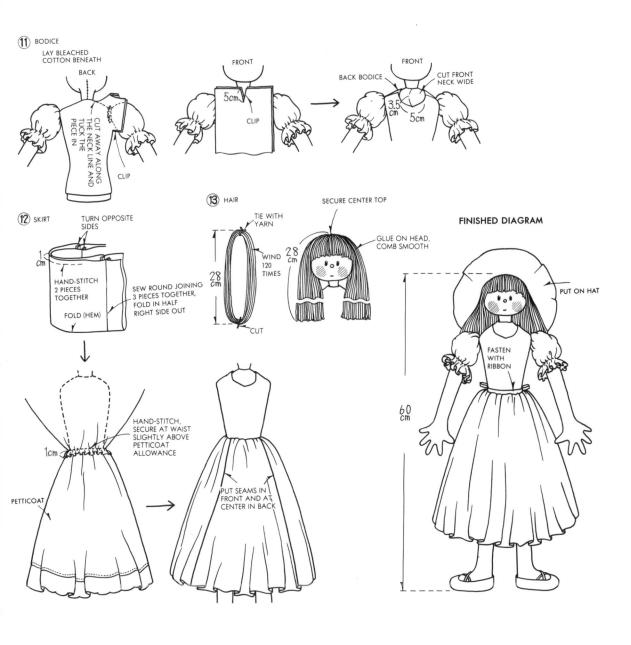

Shown on pages 4—5.

LITTLE HOUSE IN THE BIG WOODS

Use denim, calico, and homespun for an old-fashioned look for this pioneer family.

(MARY)

YOU'LL NEED:

Head-Foundation, Body, Arms, Legs—90 cm by 18 cm white rayon. Face, Nose, Arms—32 cm by 17 cm beige cotton jersey. Legs—28 cm black cotton jersey. Eyes—dacron georgette. Mouth—strands of embroidery thread. Hair—mohair yarn. Bloomer, Petticoat—60 cm by 17 cm white rayon. Skirt, Sleeves, Bonnet—63 cm by 30 cm denim. Apron-Dress—43 cm by 23 cm cotton print. Shoes—12 cm by 6 cm felt. Also—packing, cotton wadding, polyester batting.

FINISHED SIZE: Refer to diagram.

INSTRUCTIONS:

The basic method is the same as for Hiji, so refer to pages 50-64.

Make legs in same manner as for arms.

Seam sides of apron-dress, press seams open, finish the hem.

Secure hair at center of head, glue and comb smooth.

Make shoes to fit size of foot.

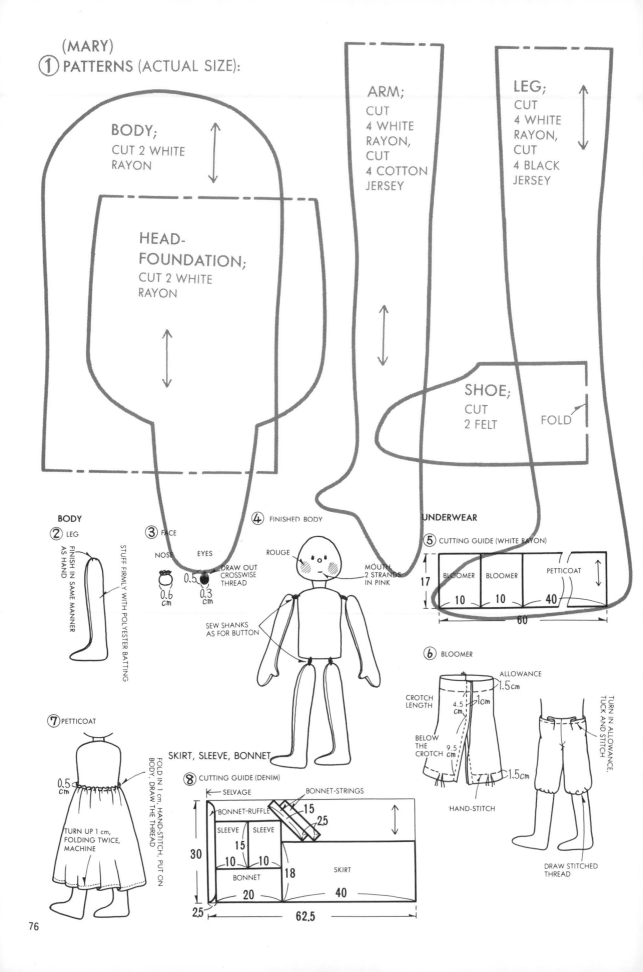

(MARY)

① PATTERNS (ACTUAL SIZE):

BODY;
CUT 2 WHITE RAYON

HEAD-FOUNDATION;
CUT 2 WHITE RAYON

ARM;
CUT 4 WHITE RAYON,
CUT 4 COTTON JERSEY

LEG;
CUT 4 WHITE RAYON,
CUT 4 BLACK JERSEY

SHOE;
CUT 2 FELT

FOLD

BODY

② LEG

FINISH IN SAME MANNER AS HAND

STUFF FIRMLY WITH POLYESTER BATTING

③ FACE

NOSE   EYES

0.6 cm   0.5   0.3 cm

DRAW OUT CROSSWISE THREAD

④ FINISHED BODY

ROUGE

MOUTH
2 STRANDS IN PINK

SEW SHANKS AS FOR BUTTON

UNDERWEAR

⑤ CUTTING GUIDE (WHITE RAYON)

BLOOMER	BLOOMER	PETTICOAT
10	10	40

17

60

⑥ BLOOMER

ALLOWANCE
1.5 cm

CROTCH LENGTH

4.5 cm   1 cm

BELOW THE CROTCH   9.5 cm

1.5 cm

HAND-STITCH

TURN IN ALLOWANCE. TUCK AND STITCH

DRAW STITCHED THREAD

⑦ PETTICOAT

FOLD IN 1 cm, HAND-STITCH, PUT ON BODY. DRAW THE THREAD

0.5 cm

TURN UP 1 cm, FOLDING TWICE, MACHINE

SKIRT, SLEEVE, BONNET

⑧ CUTTING GUIDE (DENIM)

SELVAGE

BONNET-STRINGS

BONNET-RUFFLE   15

25

SLEEVE	SLEEVE		
15			
10	10	18	SKIRT
BONNET			40

30

20

2.5

62.5

76

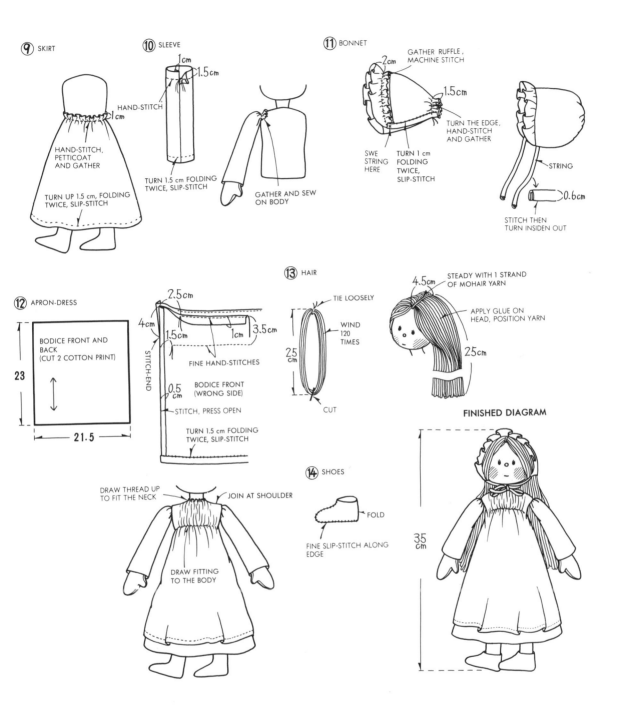

⑨ SKIRT

HAND-STITCH

HAND-STITCH, PETTICOAT AND GATHER

1 cm

TURN UP 1.5 cm, FOLDING TWICE, SLIP-STITCH

⑩ SLEEVE

1 cm

1.5 cm

HAND-STITCH

TURN 1.5 cm FOLDING TWICE, SLIP-STITCH

GATHER AND SEW ON BODY

⑪ BONNET

GATHER RUFFLE, MACHINE STITCH

2 cm

1.5 cm

TURN THE EDGE, HAND-STITCH AND GATHER

SWE STRING HERE

TURN 1 cm FOLDING TWICE, SLIP-STITCH

STRING

0.6 cm

STITCH THEN TURN INSIDEN OUT

⑫ APRON-DRESS

23

BODICE FRONT AND BACK (CUT 2 COTTON PRINT)

21.5

2.5 cm

4 cm

1.5 cm

1 cm

3.5 cm

STITCH-END

FINE HAND-STITCHES

0.5 cm

BODICE FRONT (WRONG SIDE)

STITCH, PRESS OPEN

TURN 1.5 cm FOLDING TWICE, SLIP-STITCH

⑬ HAIR

TIE LOOSELY

WIND 120 TIMES

25 cm

CUT

4.5 cm

STEADY WITH 1 STRAND OF MOHAIR YARN

APPLY GLUE ON HEAD, POSITION YARN

25 cm

FINISHED DIAGRAM

DRAW THREAD UP TO FIT THE NECK

JOIN AT SHOULDER

DRAW FITTING TO THE BODY

⑭ SHOES

FOLD

FINE SLIP-STITCH ALONG EDGE

35 cm

(LAURA)

YOU'LL NEED:

Head-Foundation, Body, Arms, Legs—84 cm by 17 cm white rayon. Face, Nose, Arms—32 cm by 15 cm beige cotton jersey. Legs—26 cm by 17 cm black cotton jersey. Eyes—dacron georgette. Mouth—strands of embroidery thread. Hair-mohair yarn. Bloomer, Petticoat—60 cm by 15 cm white rayon. Skirt—45 cm by 16 cm lightweight cotton fabric. Dress, Bonnet—67 cm by 30 cm cotton print.

Shoes—11 cm by 5.5 cm felt. Also—packing, cotton wadding, polyester batting.

FINISHED SIZE: Refer to diagram.

INSTRUCTIONS:

The basic method is the same as for Hiji, so refer to pages 50-60, and made in same manner as Mary.

Secure hair on top left side, cut the ends evenly.

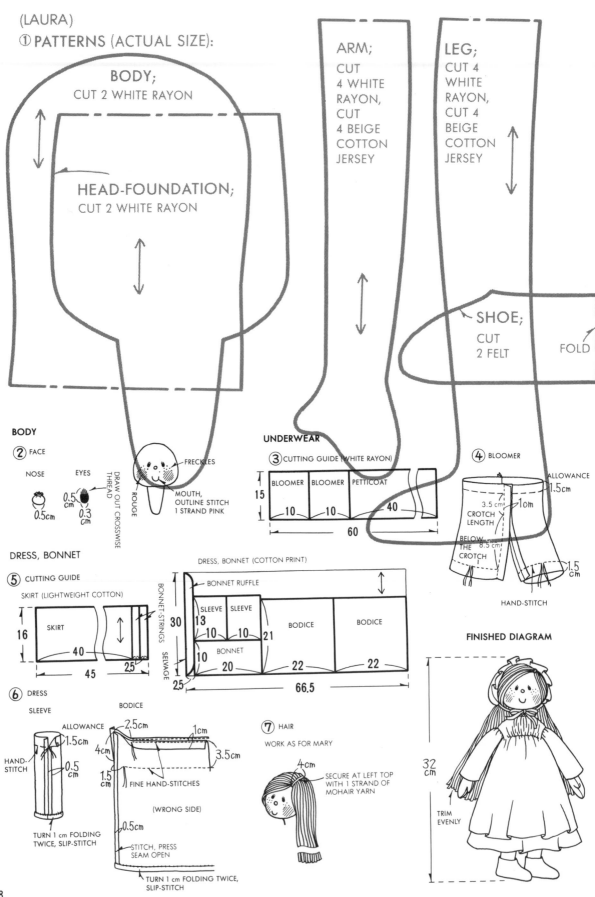

(LAURA)

① PATTERNS (ACTUAL SIZE):

BODY;
CUT 2 WHITE RAYON

HEAD-FOUNDATION;
CUT 2 WHITE RAYON

ARM;
CUT 4 WHITE RAYON,
CUT 4 BEIGE COTTON JERSEY

LEG;
CUT 4 WHITE RAYON,
CUT 4 BEIGE COTTON JERSEY

SHOE;
CUT 2 FELT

FOLD

BODY

② FACE

NOSE
0.5cm

EYES
0.5 cm
0.3 cm

DRAW OUT CROSSWISE THREAD

ROUGE

FRECKLES

MOUTH, OUTLINE STITCH 1 STRAND PINK

UNDERWEAR

③ CUTTING GUIDE (WHITE RAYON)

BLOOMER	BLOOMER	PETTICOAT
10	10	40

15

60

④ BLOOMER

ALLOWANCE 1.5cm

3.5 cm

10m

CROTCH LENGTH

BELOW THE CROTCH 8.5 cm

1.5 cm

HAND-STITCH

DRESS, BONNET

⑤ CUTTING GUIDE

SKIRT (LIGHTWEIGHT COTTON)

SKIRT
16
40
45
2.5

DRESS, BONNET (COTTON PRINT)

BONNET RUFFLE

BONNET-STRINGS

SELVAGE

SLEEVE	SLEEVE	BODICE	BODICE

13
30
10   10   21
10
BONNET
2.5   20   22   22
66.5

⑥ DRESS

SLEEVE

ALLOWANCE 1.5cm

HAND-STITCH

0.5 cm

TURN 1 cm FOLDING TWICE, SLIP-STITCH

BODICE

2.5cm

1cm

4cm

3.5cm

1.5 cm

FINE HAND-STITCHES

(WRONG SIDE)

0.5cm

STITCH, PRESS SEAM OPEN

TURN 1 cm FOLDING TWICE, SLIP-STITCH

⑦ HAIR

WORK AS FOR MARY

4cm

SECURE AT LEFT TOP WITH 1 STRAND OF MOHAIR YARN

FINISHED DIAGRAM

32 cm

TRIM EVENLY

(CARRIE)

YOU'LL NEED:

Head-Foundation, Body, Arms, Legs—60 cm by 12 cm white rayon. Face, Nose Arms, Legs—30 cm by 20 cm cotton jersey. Eyes—dacron georgette. Mouth—strands of embroidery thread. Hair—mohair yarn. Shoes—6.5 cm by 4.5 cm felt. Bloomer, Petticoat—40 cm by 9 cm white rayon. Skirt—25 cm by 10 cm lightweight cotton fabric. Dress, Bonnet—35 cm by 30 cm cotton print. Also—packing, cotton wadding, polyester batting.

FINISHED SIZE: Refer to diagram.

INSTRUCTIONS:

The basic method is the same as for Hiji, so refer to pages 50-64.

Put on shoes and stitch to fit each foot.

Make underwear, dress, and bonnet in same manner as for Mary.

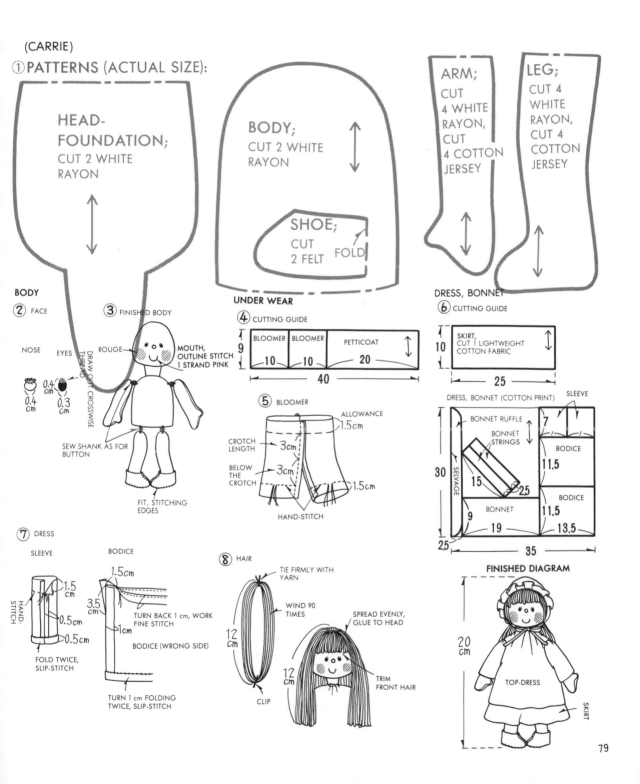

(CARRIE)

① PATTERNS (ACTUAL SIZE):

HEAD-FOUNDATION; CUT 2 WHITE RAYON

BODY; CUT 2 WHITE RAYON

SHOE; CUT 2 FELT FOLD

ARM; CUT 4 WHITE RAYON, CUT 4 COTTON JERSEY

LEG; CUT 4 WHITE RAYON, CUT 4 COTTON JERSEY

BODY

② FACE

③ FINISHED BODY

NOSE EYES ROUGE MOUTH, OUTLINE STITCH 1 STRAND PINK

DRAW OUT CROSSWISE THREAD

0.4 cm 0.4 cm 0.3 cm

SEW SHANK AS FOR BUTTON

FIT, STITCHING EDGES

UNDER WEAR

④ CUTTING GUIDE

| BLOOMER | BLOOMER | PETTICOAT |
| 10 | 10 | 20 |

9

40

⑤ BLOOMER

ALLOWANCE 1.5 cm

CROTCH LENGTH 3 cm

BELOW THE CROTCH 3 cm

1.5 cm

HAND-STITCH

DRESS, BONNET

⑥ CUTTING GUIDE

SKIRT, CUT 1 LIGHTWEIGHT COTTON FABRIC

10

25

DRESS, BONNET (COTTON PRINT) SLEEVE

BONNET RUFFLE

BONNET STRINGS

SELVAGE

30

BODICE 11.5

15 25

BONNET 9

BODICE 11.5

2.5 19 13.5

35

7

⑦ DRESS

SLEEVE

HAND-STITCH

1.5 cm

0.5 cm

0.5 cm

FOLD TWICE, SLIP-STITCH

BODICE

1.5 cm

3.5 cm

1 cm

TURN BACK 1 cm, WORK FINE STITCH

BODICE (WRONG SIDE)

TURN 1 cm FOLDING TWICE, SLIP-STITCH

⑧ HAIR

TIE FIRMLY WITH YARN

WIND 90 TIMES

12 cm

12 cm

CLIP

SPREAD EVENLY, GLUE TO HEAD

TRIM FRONT HAIR

FINISHED DIAGRAM

20 cm

TOP-DRESS

SKIRT

79

LITTLE WOMEN

Shown on pages 6-7

These very pretty hug-dolls are as alike as four sisters should be. Use different print fabrics to make them. Because the hair longer length, use wool yarn if it is available.

YOU'LL NEED:
Head-Foundation, Body, Arms, Legs—55 cm by 45 cm white rayon. Face, Nose, Arms, Legs—70 cm by 38 cm cotton jersey. Eyes—dacron georgette. Mouth—strands of embroidery thread. Hair—bouclé. Dress, Bloomer, Ribbon—67 cm by 44 cm cotton print. Also—packing, cotton wadding, polyester batting.
FINISHED SIZE: Refer to diagram.

INSTRUCTIONS;
The basic method is the same as for Hiji, so refer to pages 50-64.
Sew bloomer, sleeves, and bodice on body in turn. Fasten the yarn for hair in the middle, secure at top of head. Apply glue, attach the yarn, parted on the side, and comb smooth. Put ribbon on head.

(1) PATTERNS (ACTUAL SIZE):

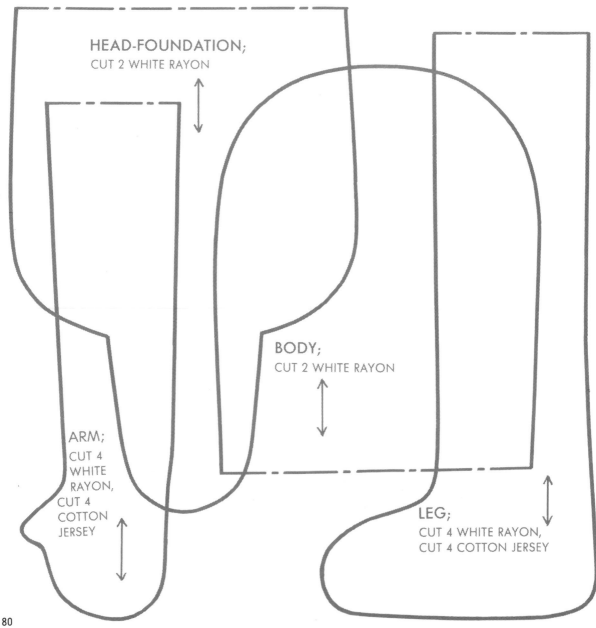

HEAD-FOUNDATION;
CUT 2 WHITE RAYON

BODY;
CUT 2 WHITE RAYON

ARM;
CUT 4 WHITE RAYON,
CUT 4 COTTON JERSEY

LEG;
CUT 4 WHITE RAYON,
CUT 4 COTTON JERSEY

BODY

② FACE

NOSE

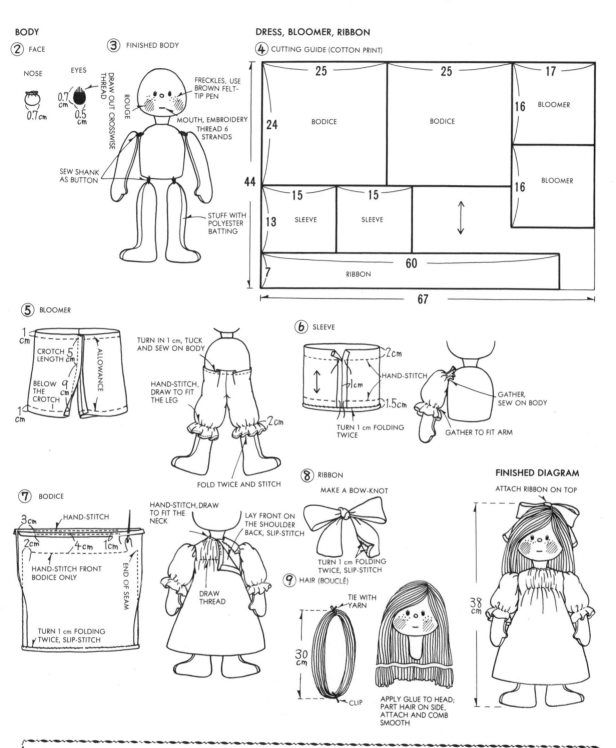

0.7cm

EYES

0.7 cm
0.5 cm

③ FINISHED BODY

DRAW OUT CROSSWISE THREAD

ROUGE

FRECKLES, USE BROWN FELT-TIP PEN

MOUTH, EMBROIDERY THREAD 6 STRANDS

SEW SHANK AS BUTTON

STUFF WITH POLYESTER BATTING

DRESS, BLOOMER, RIBBON

④ CUTTING GUIDE (COTTON PRINT)

25	25	17

24 — BODICE — BODICE — 16 — BLOOMER

44

16 — BLOOMER

| 15 | 15 | |
13 — SLEEVE — SLEEVE

7 — RIBBON — 60

67

⑤ BLOOMER

1 cm

CROTCH LENGTH 5 cm

ALLOWANCE

BELOW THE CROTCH 9 cm

1 cm

TURN IN 1 cm, TUCK AND SEW ON BODY

HAND-STITCH, DRAW TO FIT THE LEG

2 cm

FOLD TWICE AND STITCH

⑥ SLEEVE

2 cm

HAND-STITCH

1cm

TURN 1 cm FOLDING TWICE

1.5cm

GATHER, SEW ON BODY

GATHER TO FIT ARM

⑦ BODICE

3 cm

HAND-STITCH

2cm
4 cm 1cm

HAND-STITCH FRONT BODICE ONLY

END OF SEAM

TURN 1 cm FOLDING TWICE, SLIP-STITCH

HAND-STITCH, DRAW TO FIT THE NECK

LAY FRONT ON THE SHOULDER BACK, SLIP-STITCH

DRAW THREAD

⑧ RIBBON

MAKE A BOW-KNOT

TURN 1 cm FOLDING TWICE, SLIP-STITCH

⑨ HAIR (BOUCLÉ)

TIE WITH YARN

30 cm

CLIP

APPLY GLUE TO HEAD; PART HAIR ON SIDE, ATTACH AND COMB SMOOTH

FINISHED DIAGRAM

ATTACH RIBBON ON TOP

38 cm

MOTHER GOOSE

Shown on pages 8-9.

Bodies are simply made from scraps of fabric. Make individual dolls to suit the taste of each child.

(MONDAY'S CHILD)

YOU'LL NEED:

Head-Foundation—24 cm by 18 cm white rayon. Face, Nose—24 cm by 22 cm cotton jersey. Body, Arms, Skirt, Collar—21 cm by 75 cm velveteen, 110 cm of 1 cm lace.

Eyes—dacron georgette. Mouth—strands of embroidery thread. Hair—mohair yarn, 30 cm of 1 cm ribbon. Also—artificial flowers, packing, cotton wadding, polyester batting.

INSTRUCTIONS:

The basic method is the same as for Hiji, so refer to pages 50-64.

Make head-foundation and face as shown on pages 54-57.

Cut body, arms, skirt, and collar from velveteen.

Sew body leaving the opening for stuffing on back, stuff packing as firmly as possible into the top where neck is to be fixed. Then stuff polyester batting carefully beginning at toe.

Sew arm, make a slash on the inside, turn inside out and stuff with polyester batting.

Make a neck-size hole on the top of the body, apply glue, insert neck firmly into hole.

Attach hair following the steps shown on page 72.

·Use patterns below for all dolls, making head and body in this same manner.

① **PATTERNS** (ACTUAL SIZE):

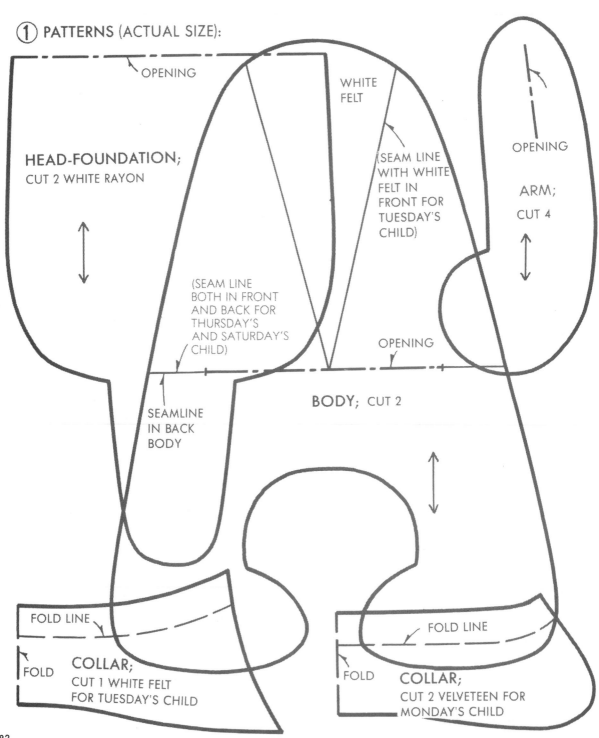

OPENING

HEAD-FOUNDATION;
CUT 2 WHITE RAYON

WHITE FELT

(SEAM LINE WITH WHITE FELT IN FRONT FOR TUESDAY'S CHILD)

OPENING

ARM;
CUT 4

(SEAM LINE BOTH IN FRONT AND BACK FOR THURSDAY'S AND SATURDAY'S CHILD)

OPENING

SEAMLINE IN BACK BODY

BODY; CUT 2

FOLD LINE

FOLD

COLLAR;
CUT 1 WHITE FELT
FOR TUESDAY'S CHILD

FOLD LINE

FOLD

COLLAR;
CUT 2 VELVETEEN FOR
MONDAY'S CHILD

BODY

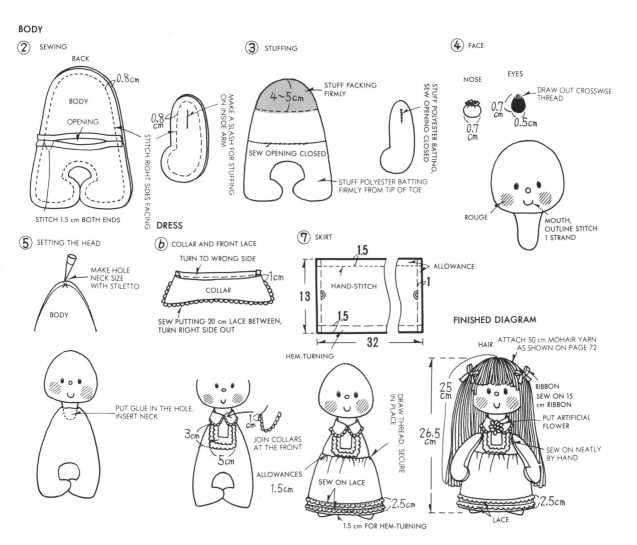

② SEWING

BACK

0.8cm

BODY

OPENING

STITCH 1.5 cm BOTH ENDS

0.8 cm

MAKE A SLASH FOR STUFFING ON INSIDE ARM

STITCH RIGHT SIDES FACING

③ STUFFING

STUFF PACKING FIRMLY

4~5cm

SEW OPENING CLOSED

STUFF POLYESTER BATTING, SEW OPENING CLOSED

STUFF POLYESTER BATTING FIRMLY FROM TIP OF TOE

④ FACE

NOSE

EYES

0.7 cm

0.7 cm   0.5cm

DRAW OUT CROSSWISE THREAD

ROUGE

MOUTH, OUTLINE STITCH 1 STRAND

DRESS

⑤ SETTING THE HEAD

MAKE HOLE NECK SIZE WITH STILETTO

BODY

⑥ COLLAR AND FRONT LACE

TURN TO WRONG SIDE

COLLAR

1cm

SEW PUTTING 20 cm LACE BETWEEN, TURN RIGHT SIDE OUT

HEM-TURNING

⑦ SKIRT

1.5

HAND-STITCH

13

1.5

32

ALLOWANCE

1

FINISHED DIAGRAM

PUT GLUE IN THE HOLE, INSERT NECK

1cm

3cm

5cm

JOIN COLLARS AT THE FRONT

ALLOWANCES 1.5cm

DRAW THREAD, SECURE IN PLACE

SEW ON LACE

2.5cm

1.5 cm FOR HEM-TURNING

HAIR   ATTACH 50 cm MOHAIR YARN AS SHOWN ON PAGE 72

25 cm

26.5 cm

RIBBON SEW ON 15 cm RIBBON

PUT ARTIFICIAL FLOWER

SEW ON NEATLY BY HAND

2.5cm

LACE

(TUESDAY'S CHILD)

YOU'LL NEED:

Head-Foundation—24 cm by 18 cm white rayon. Face, Nose —24 cm by 22 cm cotton jersey. Body, Arms—42 cm by 24 cm velveteen. Eyes—dacron georgette. Mouth—strands of embroidery thread. Hair—mohair yarn. Collar, Yoke—20 cm by 10 cm felt. Also—6cm of 5 cm ribbon, packing, cotton wadding, polyester batting.

INSTRUCTIONS;

Make in same manner as Monday's child.

Make hair winding 2 strands of yarns around 2 fingers ten times, tie with white machine thread, secure to head as shown on page 67.

FINISHED DIAGRAM

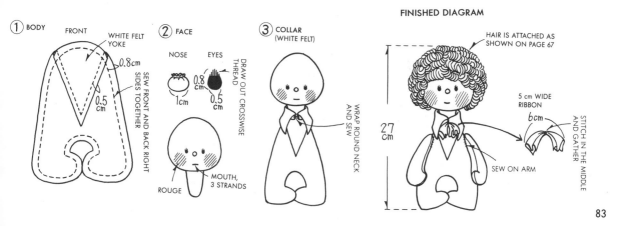

① BODY

FRONT

WHITE FELT YOKE

0.8cm

0.5 cm

SEW FRONT AND BACK RIGHT SIDES TOGETHER

② FACE

NOSE   EYES

0.8 cm   0.5 cm

1cm

DRAW OUT CROSSWISE THREAD

ROUGE

MOUTH, 3 STRANDS

③ COLLAR (WHITE FELT)

WRAP ROUND NECK AND SEW

HAIR IS ATTACHED AS SHOWN ON PAGE 67

27 cm

5 cm WIDE RIBBON

6cm

STITCH IN THE MIDDLE AND GATHER

SEW ON ARM

(WEDNESDAY'S CHILD)
YOU'LL NEED:

Head-Foundation—24 cm by 18 cm white rayon. Face, Nose—24 cm by 22 cm cotton jersey. Body, Arms, Skirt—72 cm by 24 cm velveteen. Eyes—dacron georgette. Mouth—strands of embroidery thread. Hair—mohair yarn. Apron, Cap—65 cm by 25 cm lightweight cotton fabric, 66 cm of 1.5 cm lace. Also—1.3 cm diameter button, 15 cm of 1.5

cm lace, packing, cotton wadding, polyester batting.
INSTRUCTIONS:
Make in same manner as Monday's child.
Make cap and apron.
Wrap lace round the neck, secure with button.

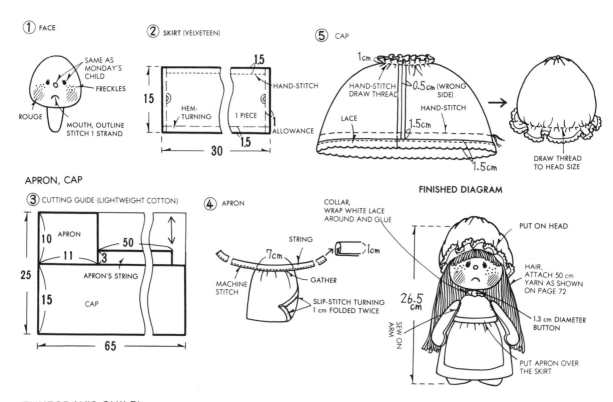

APRON, CAP

FINISHED DIAGRAM

(THURSDAY'S CHILD)
YOU'LL NEED:

Head-Foundation—24 cm by 18 cm white rayon. Face, Nose—24 cm by 22 cm cotton jersey. Body, Arms—52 cm by 12 cm velveteen. Legs—30 cm by 11 cm corduroy. Eyes—dacron georgette. Mouth—strands of embroidery thread. Hair—mohair yarn. Scarf—15 cm by 15 cm wool. Cap, Suitcase—Heavyweight yarn. Also—3 of 0.8 cm diameter

button, packing, cotton wadding, polyester batting.
INSTRUCTIONS;
Make in same manner as Monday's child.
Crochet cap with No. F crochet hook, and put on head.
Crochet suitcase with same yarn as cap.

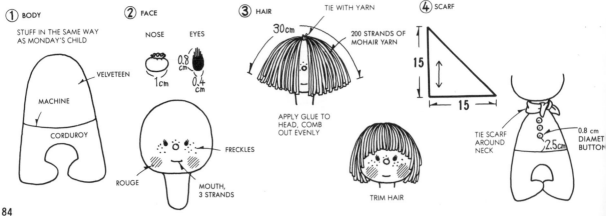

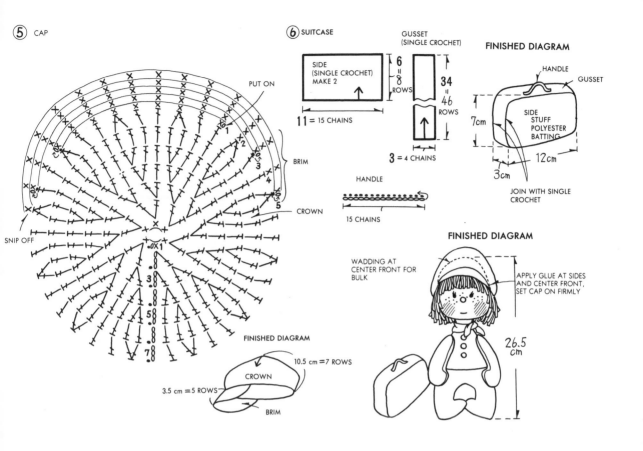

⑤ CAP

PUT ON

BRIM

CROWN

SNIP OFF

⑥ SUITCASE

SIDE
(SINGLE CROCHET)
MAKE 2

11 = 15 CHAINS

GUSSET
(SINGLE CROCHET)

6
=
8
ROWS

34
=
46
ROWS

3 = 4 CHAINS

HANDLE

15 CHAINS

FINISHED DIAGRAM

HANDLE

GUSSET

SIDE
STUFF
POLYESTER
BATTING

7cm

3cm

12cm

JOIN WITH SINGLE
CROCHET

FINISHED DIAGRAM

CROWN

BRIM

10.5 cm = 7 ROWS

3.5 cm = 5 ROWS

FINISHED DIAGRAM

WADDING AT
CENTER FRONT FOR
BULK

APPLY GLUE AT SIDES
AND CENTER FRONT,
SET CAP ON FIRMLY

26.5
cm

(FRIDAY'S CHILD)

YOU'LL NEED:
Head-Foundation—24 cm by 18 cm white rayon. Face,
Nose—24 cm by 22 cm cotton jersey. Body, Skirt, Arms,
Ribbon—80 cm by 19 cm velveten. Eyes—dacron georgette.
Mouth—strands of embroidery thread. Hair—mohair yarn.
Stole, Hair-Band—Lightweight yarn. Also—packing, cotton
wadding, polyester bating.

INSTRUCTIONS:
Make in same manner as Monday's child.
Crochet hair-band and stole with No. 4 hook.

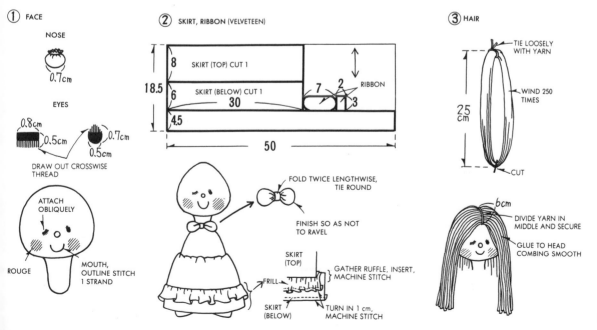

① FACE

NOSE

0.7cm

EYES

0.8cm
0.5cm
0.7cm
0.5cm

DRAW OUT CROSSWISE
THREAD

ATTACH
OBLIQUELY

ROUGE

MOUTH,
OUTLINE STITCH
1 STRAND

② SKIRT, RIBBON (VELVETEEN)

8 SKIRT (TOP) CUT 1

18.5

6 SKIRT (BELOW) CUT 1

30

7 2
3 RIBBON

4.5

50

FOLD TWICE LENGTHWISE,
TIE ROUND

FINISH SO AS NOT
TO RAVEL

SKIRT
(TOP)

FRILL

SKIRT
(BELOW)

GATHER RUFFLE, INSERT,
MACHINE STITCH

TURN IN 1 cm,
MACHINE STITCH

③ HAIR

TIE LOOSELY
WITH YARN

WIND 250
TIMES

25
cm

CUT

6cm

DIVIDE YARN IN
MIDDLE AND SECURE

GLUE TO HEAD
COMBING SMOOTH

85

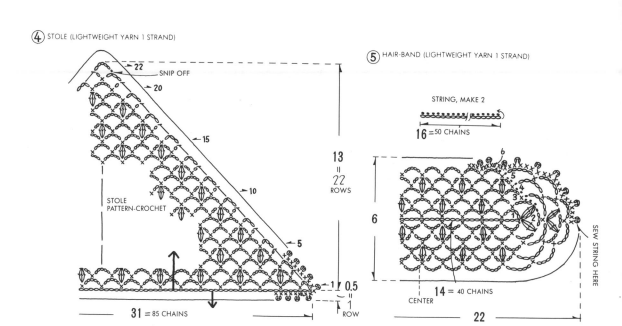

④ STOLE (LIGHTWEIGHT YARN 1 STRAND)

22
SNIP OFF
20
15
STOLE PATTERN-CROCHET
10
5
1 — 0.5
1 ROW
13 = 22 ROWS
31 = 85 CHAINS

⑤ HAIR-BAND (LIGHTWEIGHT YARN 1 STRAND)

STRING, MAKE 2
16 = 50 CHAINS

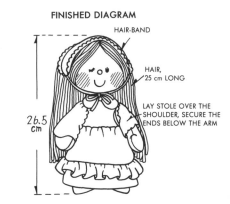

6
14 = 40 CHAINS
CENTER
22
SEW STRING HERE

FINISHED DIAGRAM

HAIR-BAND
HAIR, 25 cm LONG
LAY STOLE OVER THE SHOULDER, SECURE THE ENDS BELOW THE ARM
26.5 cm

(SATURDAY'S CHILD)

YOU'LL NEED:

Head-Foundation—24 cm by 18 cm white rayon. Face, Nose—24 cm by 22 cm cotton jersey. Body, Arms, Collar—52 cm by 20 cm velveteen. Legs —30 cm by 11 cm striped velveteen. Eyes—dacron georgette. Mouth— strands of embroidery thread. Hair—mohair yarn. Also—30 cm of 1 cm braid, 30 cm square gauze, packing, cotton wadding, polyester batting.

INSTRUCTIONS:

Cut out top and pants of body from different fabrics.
Make in same manner as Monday's child.
Sew hair of yarn all over head, without clipping.

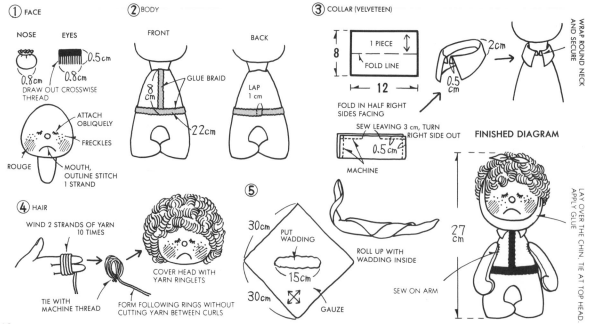

① FACE

NOSE   EYES
0.5cm
0.8cm   0.8cm
DRAW OUT CROSSWISE THREAD

ATTACH OBLIQUELY
FRECKLES
ROUGE
MOUTH, OUTLINE STITCH 1 STRAND

② BODY

FRONT   BACK
GLUE BRAID
8 cm
22cm
LAP 1 cm

③ COLLAR (VELVETEEN)

8
1 PIECE
FOLD LINE
12
FOLD IN HALF RIGHT SIDES FACING
SEW LEAVING 3 cm, TURN RIGHT SIDE OUT
0.5 cm
MACHINE
2cm
0.5 cm
WRAP ROUND NECK AND SECURE

FINISHED DIAGRAM

④ HAIR

WIND 2 STRANDS OF YARN 10 TIMES
TIE WITH MACHINE THREAD
COVER HEAD WITH YARN RINGLETS
FORM FOLLOWING RINGS WITHOUT CUTTING YARN BETWEEN CURLS

⑤
30cm
PUT WADDING
15cm
30cm
GAUZE
ROLL UP WITH WADDING INSIDE

27 cm
SEW ON ARM
LAY OVER THE CHIN, TIE AT TOP HEAD. APPLY GLUE

(SUNDAY'S CHILD)

YOU'LL NEED:
Head-Foundation—24 cm by 18 cm white rayon. Face, Nose—24 cm by 22 cm cotton jersey. Body, Arms, Skirt, Hood—75 cm by 26 cm velvetten. Eyes—dacron georgette. Mouth—strands of embroidery thread. Hair—mohair yarn. Apron—35 cm by 11 cm lightweight cotton fabric. Also—

100 cm of 1.5 cm lace, 10 cm of 0.5 cm ribbon, packing, cotton wadding, polyester batting.

INSTRUCTIONS:
Make in same manner as Monday's child. Sew on apron and attach hood.

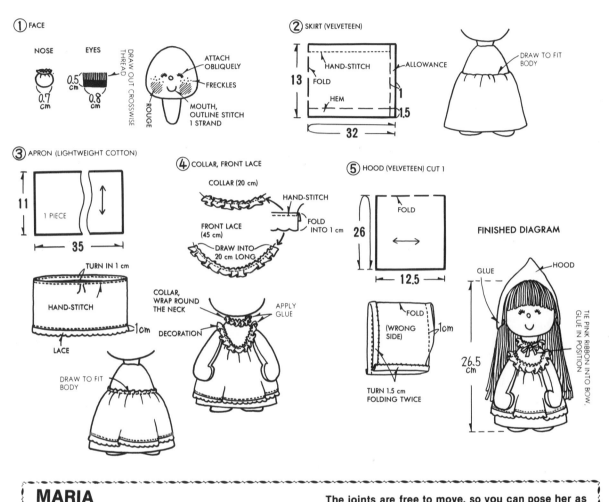

① FACE — NOSE, EYES 0.5 cm, 0.7 cm, 0.8 cm, DRAW OUT CROSSWISE THREAD, ROUGE, ATTACH OBLIQUELY, FRECKLES, MOUTH, OUTLINE STITCH 1 STRAND

② SKIRT (VELVETEEN) — HAND-STITCH, ALLOWANCE, 13, FOLD, HEM, 32, 1.5, DRAW TO FIT BODY

③ APRON (LIGHTWEIGHT COTTON) — 11, 1 PIECE, 35, TURN IN 1 cm, HAND-STITCH, 1cm, LACE, DRAW TO FIT BODY

④ COLLAR, FRONT LACE — COLLAR (20 cm), HAND-STITCH, FOLD INTO 1 cm, FRONT LACE (45 cm), DRAW INTO 20 cm LONG, COLLAR, WRAP ROUND THE NECK, DECORATION, APPLY GLUE

⑤ HOOD (VELVETEEN) CUT 1 — FOLD, 26, 12.5, FOLD (WRONG SIDE), 1cm, TURN 1.5 cm FOLDING TWICE

FINISHED DIAGRAM — GLUE, HOOD, 26.5 cm, TIE PINK RIBBON INTO BOW, GLUE IN POSITION

MARIA

Shown on page 10.

The joints are free to move, so you can pose her as you like. The body of such a tall and thin doll needs to be finished firmly with packing.

YOU'LL NEED:
Head-Foundation, Body, Arms, Legs—90 cm by 55 cm white rayon. Face, Nose, Arms—90 cm by 30 cm beige georgette. Legs—70 cm by 27 cm white georgette. Eyes—dacron georgette. Mounth—strands of embroidery thread. Hair—sport weitht yarn. Bloomer, Petticoat—85 cm by 34 cm broadcloth, 130 cm of 5 cm lace. Skirt—80 cm by 40 cm cotton print. Apron—28 cm by 35 cm crepe. Sleeves, Bodice —62 cm by 30 cm lace fabric, 80 cm of 3.5 cm lace. Vest—30 cm by 17 cm black felt, 40 cm of 1 cm tyrolean braid. Shoes—22 cm by 16 cm lightweight cotton fabric, 8 cm by 6 cm brown felt. Also—packing, cotton wadding, polyester

batting.

FINISHED SIZE: 74 cm tall.

INSTRUCTIONS
The basic method is the same as for Hiji, so refer to pages 50-64.
Make arms and legs that can be bent freely.
Cut fabric shoe pieces on bias and sew on.
Sew bodice front and back on neatly. Put vest on in same manner as bodice.
Make hair of yarn, glue on head and trim.

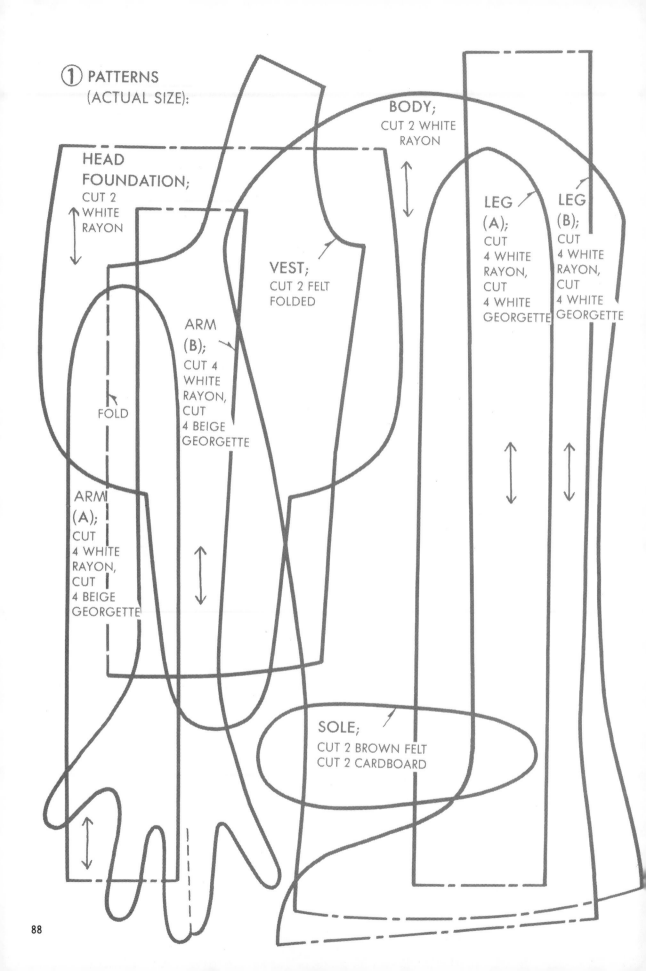

① PATTERNS
(ACTUAL SIZE):

HEAD
FOUNDATION;
CUT 2
WHITE
RAYON

BODY;
CUT 2 WHITE
RAYON

VEST;
CUT 2 FELT
FOLDED

LEG
(A);
CUT
4 WHITE
RAYON,
CUT
4 WHITE
GEORGETTE

LEG
(B);
CUT
4 WHITE
RAYON,
CUT
4 WHITE
GEORGETTE

ARM
(B);
CUT 4
WHITE
RAYON,
CUT
4 BEIGE
GEORGETTE

FOLD

ARM
(A);
CUT
4 WHITE
RAYON,
CUT
4 BEIGE
GEORGETTE

SOLE;
CUT 2 BROWN FELT
CUT 2 CARDBOARD

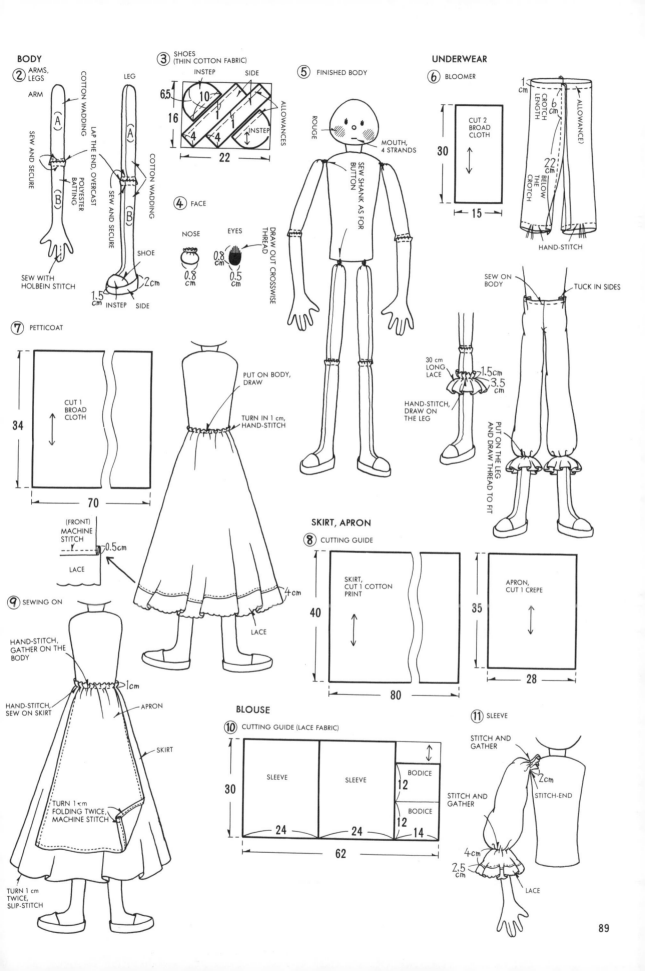

BODY

② ARMS, LEGS

ARM

COTTON WADDING

SEW AND SECURE

POLYESTER BATTING

LAP THE END, OVERCAST

(A)

(B)

SEW WITH HOLBEIN STITCH

LEG

COTTON WADDING

SEW AND SECURE

(A)

COTTON WADDING

(B)

SHOE

2cm

1.5 cm

INSTEP   SIDE

③ SHOES (THIN COTTON FABRIC)

INSTEP   SIDE

6.5

16

10

1

1

4   4

INSTEP

ALLOWANCES

22

④ FACE

NOSE

0.8 cm

0.8 cm

EYES

0.8 cm

0.5 cm

DRAW OUT CROSSWISE THREAD

⑤ FINISHED BODY

ROUGE

MOUTH, 4 STRANDS

SEW SHANK AS FOR BUTTON

UNDERWEAR

⑥ BLOOMER

CUT 2 BROAD CLOTH

30

15

1 cm

CROTCH LENGTH

6 cm

ALLOWANCE)

22 cm BELOW THE CROTCH

HAND-STITCH

SEW ON BODY

TUCK IN SIDES

30 cm LONG LACE

1.5cm

3.5 cm

HAND-STITCH, DRAW ON THE LEG

PUT ON THE LEG AND DRAW THREAD TO FIT

⑦ PETTICOAT

CUT 1 BROAD CLOTH

34

70

PUT ON BODY, DRAW

TURN IN 1 cm, HAND-STITCH

(FRONT) MACHINE STITCH

0.5cm

LACE

4cm

LACE

SKIRT, APRON

⑧ CUTTING GUIDE

SKIRT, CUT 1 COTTON PRINT

40

80

APRON, CUT 1 CREPE

35

28

⑨ SEWING ON

HAND-STITCH, GATHER ON THE BODY

HAND-STITCH, SEW ON SKIRT

1cm

APRON

SKIRT

TURN 1 cm FOLDING TWICE, MACHINE STITCH

TURN 1 cm TWICE, SLIP-STITCH

BLOUSE

⑩ CUTTING GUIDE (LACE FABRIC)

30

SLEEVE

24

SLEEVE

24

BODICE

12

BODICE

12

14

62

⑪ SLEEVE

STITCH AND GATHER

2cm

STITCH-END

STITCH AND GATHER

4cm

2.5 cm

LACE

89

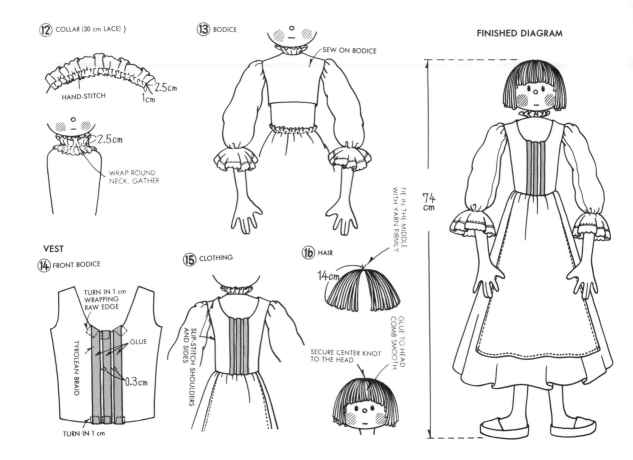

⑫ COLLAR (30 cm LACE))

HAND-STITCH 2.5cm 1cm

2.5cm

WRAP ROUND NECK, GATHER

⑬ BODICE

SEW ON BODICE

TIE IN THE MIDDLE WITH YARN FIRMLY

74 cm

FINISHED DIAGRAM

VEST

⑭ FRONT BODICE

TURN IN 1 cm WRAPPING RAW EDGE

GLUE

TYROLEAN BRAID

0.3 cm

TURN IN 1 cm

⑮ CLOTHING

SLIP-STITCH SHOULDERS AND SIDES

⑯ HAIR

14cm

GLUE TO HEAD COMB SMOOTH

SECURE CENTER KNOT TO THE HEAD

ELIZA

Shown on page 11.

Use Maria's patterns. Try to image the town of London in winter. Make a carefree girl selling flowers at the market there.

YOU'LL NEED:

Head-Foundation, Body, Arms, Legs—90 cm by 55 cm white rayon. Face, Nose, Arms—90 cm by 30 cm beige georgette. Legs—70 cm by 27 cm black woolly nylon. Eyes—dacron georgette. Mouth—strands of embroidery thread. Hair—mohair yarn. Bloomer, Petticoat—85 cm by 34 cm broadcloth, 130 cm of 5 cm lace. Suit—92 cm by 56 cm velveteen. Blouse—46 cm by 34 cm crepe. Apron—80 cm by 40 cm cotton print. Scarf—23 cm by 23 cm georgette. Hat—black heavyweight yarn, 30 cm of 0.6 cm grosgrain ribbon, artificial flowers. Stole, Bag—frizzy yarn, Artificial flower. Shoes—18 cm by 13 cm corduroy. Also—packing, cotton wadding, polyester batting.

FINISHED, SIZE: Refer to diagram.

INSTRUCTIONS:

For the body, use Maria's pattern onpage 88, and make according to the basic instructions on pages 50-64.

Use black woolly nylon for leg fabric.

For the hair, make 80 cm long skein of yarn and sew on in same manner as Hiji, braid the yarn on sides.

Crochet hat, sew on a bunch of flowers.

Crochet stole with 1 strand, bag with 2 strands, and put a bunch of flowers inside the bag.

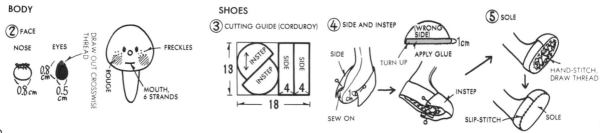

BODY

② FACE

NOSE   EYES

0.8 cm   0.8 cm   0.5 cm

DRAW OUT CROSSWISE THREAD

ROUGE

FRECKLES

MOUTH, 6 STRANDS

SHOES

③ CUTTING GUIDE (CORDUROY)

13   INSTEP   INSTEP   SIDE   SIDE   4   4

18

④ SIDE AND INSTEP

SIDE

(WRONG SIDE)

TURN UP   APPLY GLUE   1cm

INSTEP

SEW ON

⑤ SOLE

HAND-STITCH, DRAW THREAD

SLIP-STITCH   SOLE

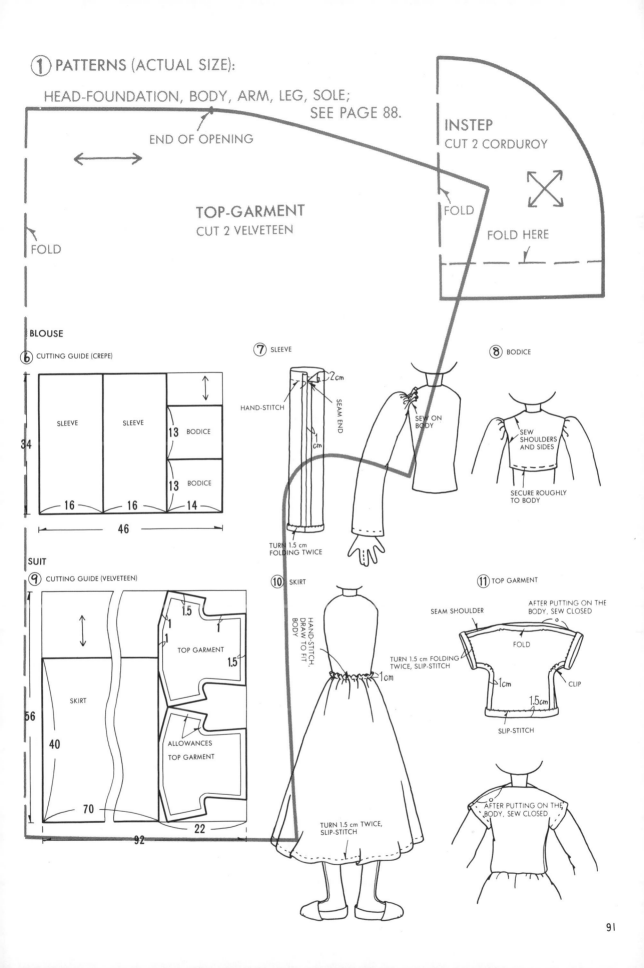

① PATTERNS (ACTUAL SIZE):

HEAD-FOUNDATION, BODY, ARM, LEG, SOLE;
SEE PAGE 88.

END OF OPENING

INSTEP
CUT 2 CORDUROY

FOLD

FOLD HERE

TOP-GARMENT
CUT 2 VELVETEEN

FOLD

BLOUSE

⑥ CUTTING GUIDE (CREPE)

34

SLEEVE | SLEEVE | 13 BODICE

13 BODICE

16 | 16 | 14

46

⑦ SLEEVE

2cm

HAND-STITCH

SEAM END

1 cm

SEW ON BODY

TURN 1.5 cm FOLDING TWICE

⑧ BODICE

SEW SHOULDERS AND SIDES

SECURE ROUGHLY TO BODY

SUIT

⑨ CUTTING GUIDE (VELVETEEN)

1.5

1 | 1

1 | TOP GARMENT | 1.5

56

SKIRT

40

ALLOWANCES TOP GARMENT

70

22

92

⑩ SKIRT

HAND-STITCH. DRAW TO FIT BODY

1 cm

TURN 1.5 cm TWICE, SLIP-STITCH

⑪ TOP GARMENT

SEAM SHOULDER

AFTER PUTTING ON THE BODY, SEW CLOSED

FOLD

TURN 1.5 cm FOLDING TWICE, SLIP-STITCH

1 cm

CLIP

1.5 cm

SLIP-STITCH

AFTER PUTTING ON THE BODY, SEW CLOSED

APRON

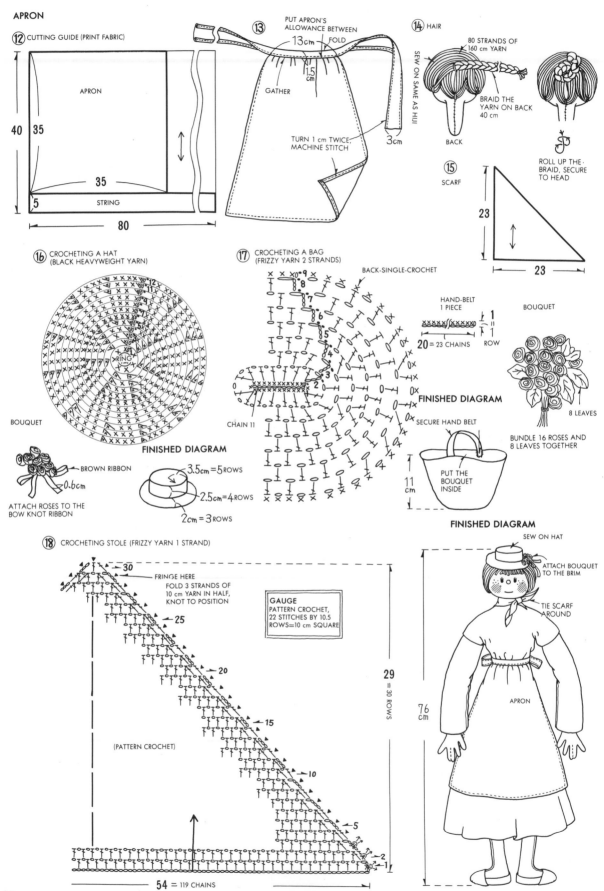

⑫ CUTTING GUIDE (PRINT FABRIC)

APRON

40
35

35

STRING
5

80

⑬ PUT APRON'S ALLOWANCE BETWEEN
FOLD
13cm
1.5 cm
GATHER
TURN 1 cm TWICE; MACHINE STITCH
3cm

⑭ HAIR
80 STRANDS OF 160 cm YARN
SEW ON SAME AS HIJI
BACK
BRAID THE YARN ON BACK 40 cm

ROLL UP THE BRAID, SECURE TO HEAD

⑮ SCARF
23
23

⑯ CROCHETING A HAT
(BLACK HEAVYWEIGHT YARN)

RING

BOUQUET

BROWN RIBBON
0.6cm

ATTACH ROSES TO THE BOW KNOT RIBBON

FINISHED DIAGRAM
3.5cm = 5 ROWS
2.5cm = 4 ROWS
2cm = 3 ROWS

⑰ CROCHETING A BAG
(FRIZZY YARN 2 STRANDS)

BACK-SINGLE-CROCHET

CHAIN 11

HAND-BELT 1 PIECE
20 = 23 CHAINS
ROW

FINISHED DIAGRAM

SECURE HAND BELT

11 cm

PUT THE BOUQUET INSIDE

BOUQUET

8 LEAVES

BUNDLE 16 ROSES AND 8 LEAVES TOGETHER

FINISHED DIAGRAM

⑱ CROCHETING STOLE (FRIZZY YARN 1 STRAND)

30
FRINGE HERE
FOLD 3 STRANDS OF 10 cm YARN IN HALF, KNOT TO POSITION
25
20

GAUGE
PATTERN CROCHET, 22 STITCHES BY 10.5 ROWS = 10 cm SQUARE

15

(PATTERN CROCHET)

10

5

2
1

29 = 30 ROWS

54 = 119 CHAINS

SEW ON HAT

ATTACH BOUQUET TO THE BRIM

TIE SCARF AROUND

APRON

76 cm

92

ROSALIE

Shown on page 12.

This is a hug-doll like Hiji and easily made. Use colored tatting thread as hair, clipping skeins in the middle.

YOU'LL NEED:

Head-Foundation, Body, Arms, Legs—50 cm by 30 cm white rayon. Face, Nose, Arms, Legs—40 cm by 27 cm beige georgette. Eyes—dacron georgette. Mouth—strands of embroidery thread. Hair—3 skeins of pink tatting thread, 50 cm of 0.5 cm ribbon. Bloomer, Petticoat—65 cm by 14 cm broadcloth, 35 cm of 1.8 cm lace. Skirt, Bodice—45 cm by 60 cm cotton print. Sleeves, Apron—52 cm by 12 cm lawn, 10 cm of 2.5 cm lace. Also—packing, cotton wadding, polyester batting.

FINISHED SIZE: Refer to diagram.

INSTRUCTIONS:

The basic method is the same as for Hiji, so refer to pages 50-64.

Stuff legs with polyester batting and finish in the same way as arms.

Attach hair as shown on page 72.

Use selvage side for the skirt ruffle, but if not available, finish cut edges by folding twice.

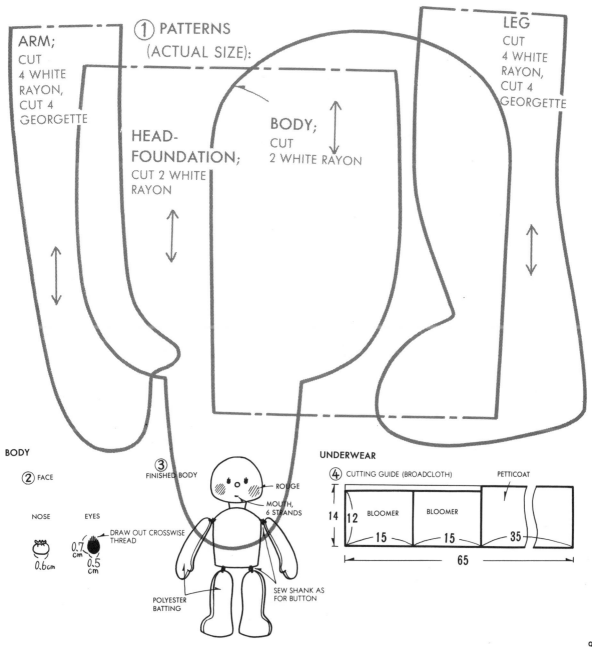

① PATTERNS (ACTUAL SIZE):

ARM;
CUT 4 WHITE RAYON, CUT 4 GEORGETTE

HEAD-FOUNDATION;
CUT 2 WHITE RAYON

BODY;
CUT 2 WHITE RAYON

LEG
CUT 4 WHITE RAYON, CUT 4 GEORGETTE

BODY

② FACE

③ FINISHED BODY

ROUGE

MOUTH, 6 STRANDS

NOSE

0.6cm

EYES

0.7 cm

0.5 cm

DRAW OUT CROSSWISE THREAD

POLYESTER BATTING

SEW SHANK AS FOR BUTTON

UNDERWEAR

④ CUTTING GUIDE (BROADCLOTH)

PETTICOAT

14

12

BLOOMER

15

BLOOMER

15

35

65

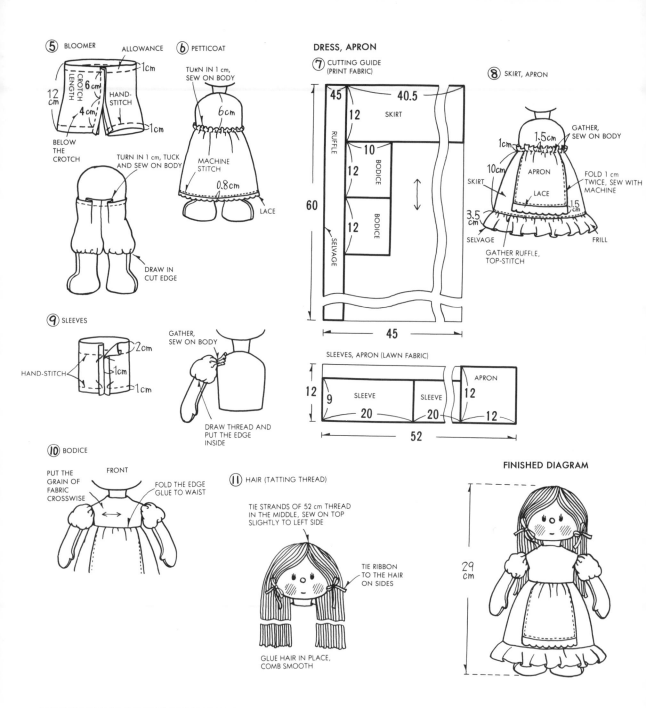

⑤ BLOOMER — ALLOWANCE — 1cm

CROTCH LENGTH · 6cm · HAND-STITCH · 12 cm · 4 cm · 1cm

BELOW THE CROTCH

TURN IN 1 cm, TUCK AND SEW ON BODY

DRAW IN CUT EDGE

⑥ PETTICOAT

TURN IN 1 cm, SEW ON BODY · 6cm

MACHINE STITCH · 0.8cm · LACE

DRESS, APRON

⑦ CUTTING GUIDE (PRINT FABRIC)

45 · 40.5 · SKIRT · 12 · RUFFLE · 10 · BODICE · 12 · BODICE · 12 · 60 · SELVAGE · 45

⑧ SKIRT, APRON

GATHER, SEW ON BODY · 1.5cm · 1cm · SKIRT · 10cm · APRON · LACE · FOLD 1 cm TWICE, SEW WITH MACHINE · 1.5 cm · 3.5 cm · SELVAGE · GATHER RUFFLE, TOP-STITCH · FRILL

⑨ SLEEVES

HAND-STITCH · 2cm · 1cm · 1cm

GATHER, SEW ON BODY

DRAW THREAD AND PUT THE EDGE INSIDE

SLEEVES, APRON (LAWN FABRIC)

12 · 9 · SLEEVE · 20 · SLEEVE · 20 · APRON · 12 · 12 · 52

⑩ BODICE

PUT THE GRAIN OF FABRIC CROSSWISE · FRONT · FOLD THE EDGE GLUE TO WAIST

⑪ HAIR (TATTING THREAD)

TIE STRANDS OF 52 cm THREAD IN THE MIDDLE, SEW ON TOP SLIGHTLY TO LEFT SIDE

TIE RIBBON TO THE HAIR ON SIDES

GLUE HAIR IN PLACE, COMB SMOOTH

FINISHED DIAGRAM

29 cm

ELLEN

Shown on page 13.

This doll, with hair that is taffy colored, is ready to go to sleep in her nightgown, so use a soft pastel fabric to express this quiet time of day.

YOU'LL NEED:
Head-Foundation, Body, Arms, Legs—70 cm by 45 cm white rayon. Face, Nose, Arms, Legs—60 cm by 30 cm beige georgette. Eyes—dacron georgette. Mouth—strands of embroidery thread. Hair—3 skeins of tatting thread. Nightcap, Nightgown, Bloomer—90 cm by 70 cm cotton print, 340 cm of 2.5 cm lace, 35 cm of 0.5 cm ribbon. Slipper—30 cm by 12 cm felt. Also—packing, cotton wadding, polyester batting.

FINISHED SIZE: Refer to diagram.
INSTRUCTIONS:
The basic method is the same as for Hiji, so refer to pages 50-64.
Make feet, putting cardboard in soles in same manner as for Hiji, sew on instep and soles of slipper. Put on nightgown after the skirt is stitched to the body. Sew on hair as shown on page 72, set on nightcap.

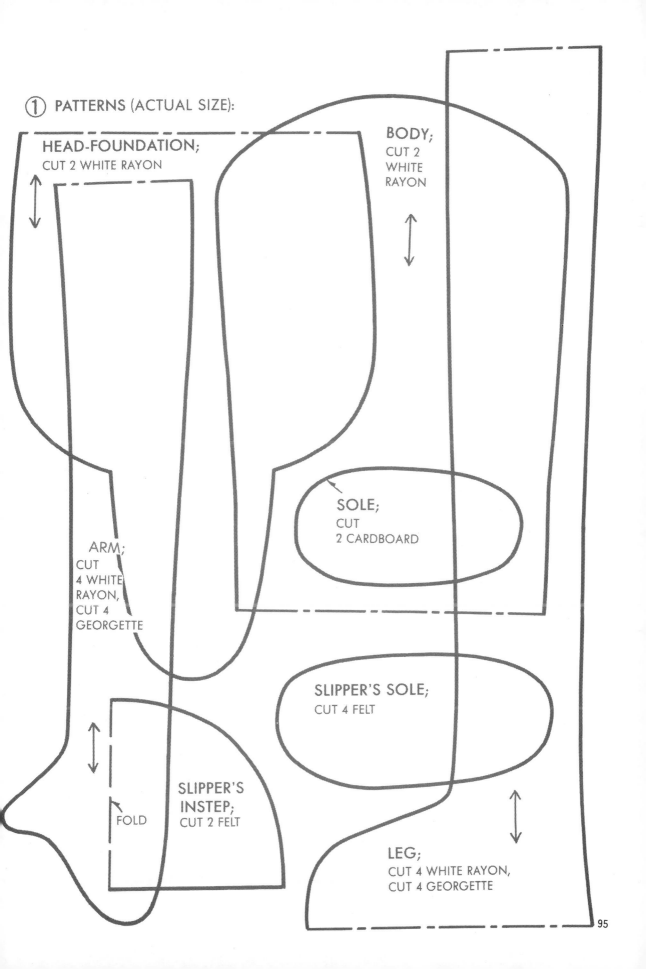

① PATTERNS (ACTUAL SIZE):

HEAD-FOUNDATION;
CUT 2 WHITE RAYON

BODY;
CUT 2
WHITE
RAYON

ARM;
CUT
4 WHITE
RAYON,
CUT 4
GEORGETTE

SOLE;
CUT
2 CARDBOARD

SLIPPER'S SOLE;
CUT 4 FELT

SLIPPER'S
INSTEP;
CUT 2 FELT

FOLD

LEG;
CUT 4 WHITE RAYON,
CUT 4 GEORGETTE

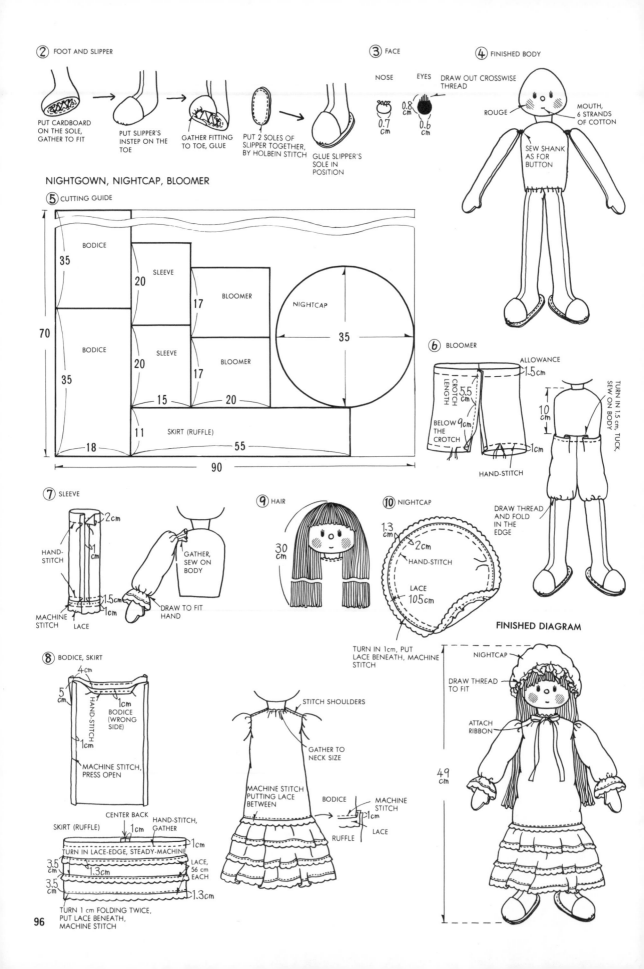

② FOOT AND SLIPPER

PUT CARDBOARD ON THE SOLE, GATHER TO FIT

PUT SLIPPER'S INSTEP ON THE TOE

GATHER FITTING TO TOE, GLUE

PUT 2 SOLES OF SLIPPER TOGETHER, BY HOLBEIN STITCH

GLUE SLIPPER'S SOLE IN POSITION

③ FACE

NOSE
0.7 cm

EYES
0.8 cm
0.6 cm

④ FINISHED BODY

DRAW OUT CROSSWISE THREAD

ROUGE

MOUTH, 6 STRANDS OF COTTON

SEW SHANK AS FOR BUTTON

NIGHTGOWN, NIGHTCAP, BLOOMER

⑤ CUTTING GUIDE

BODICE
35

SLEEVE
20

BLOOMER
17

NIGHTCAP
35

70

BODICE
35

SLEEVE
20

BLOOMER
17

15   20

11   SKIRT (RUFFLE)

18   55

90

⑥ BLOOMER

ALLOWANCE 1.5cm

CROTCH LENGTH 5.5 cm

BELOW THE CROTCH 9 cm

HAND-STITCH

1cm

TURN IN 1.5 cm, SEW ON BODY, TUCK.

10 cm

DRAW THREAD AND FOLD IN THE EDGE

⑦ SLEEVE

2cm
1cm

HAND-STITCH

1.5cm
1cm

MACHINE STITCH   LACE

GATHER, SEW ON BODY

DRAW TO FIT HAND

⑨ HAIR

30 cm

⑩ NIGHTCAP

1.3 cm
2cm
HAND-STITCH

LACE 105cm

FINISHED DIAGRAM

TURN IN 1cm, PUT LACE BENEATH, MACHINE STITCH

NIGHTCAP

DRAW THREAD TO FIT

ATTACH RIBBON

49 cm

⑧ BODICE, SKIRT

4cm
5 cm
1cm
BODICE (WRONG SIDE)

HAND-STITCH

1cm

MACHINE STITCH, PRESS OPEN

STITCH SHOULDERS

GATHER TO NECK SIZE

MACHINE STITCH PUTTING LACE BETWEEN

BODICE   MACHINE STITCH
1cm

RUFFLE   LACE

SKIRT (RUFFLE)

CENTER BACK 1cm

HAND-STITCH, GATHER

1cm

TURN IN LACE-EDGE, STEADY-MACHINE

3.5 cm   1.3cm   LACE, 56 cm EACH

3.5 cm

1.3cm

TURN 1 cm FOLDING TWICE, PUT LACE BENEATH, MACHINE STITCH

96

MAYU

Shown on page 14.

Use new-born baby socks instead of shoes, and since the top of the arms and legs have to be stuffed thicker than the opening, use polyester batting instead of wadding.

YOU'LL NEED:
Head-Foundation, Body, Arms, Legs—90 cm by 65 cm white rayon. Face, Nose, Arms—dacron georgette. Mouth—strands of embroidery thread. Hair—sport-weight yarn, 60 cm of 0.6 cm ribbon. Bloomer, Dress—90 cm by 30 cm cotton print, 18 cm by 14 cm broadcloth, 70 cm of 3 cm lace, 1.5 cm diameter button. Also—new-born baby socks, packing, cotton wadding, polyester batting.

FINISHED SIZE: Refer to diagram.
INSTRUCTIONS;
The basic method is the same as for Hiji, so refer to pages 50-64.

Legs are finished in the same way as arms, by stuffing with polyster batting. Sew on front bodice after lace is stitched to the yoke.

Sew on hair same as Hiji's braid the sides, loop the braids and secure with ribbons.

HEAD-FOUNDATION
CUT 2 WHITE RAYON

ARM;
CUT 4
WHITE
RAYON,
CUT 4
GEORGETTE

① PATTERNS
(ACTUAL SIZE)

FRONT YOKE;
CUT 1 CENTER
FOLDED BROAD-
CLOTH

BODY;
CUT 2
WHITE
RAYON

FOLD

LEG;
CUT 4 WHITE RAYON,
CUT 4 GEORGETTE

FRONT
BODICE;
CUT 1
CENTER
FOLDED
PRINT FABRIC

FOLD

COLLAR;
CUT 2 CENTER
FOLDED BROAD-
CLOTH

FOLD

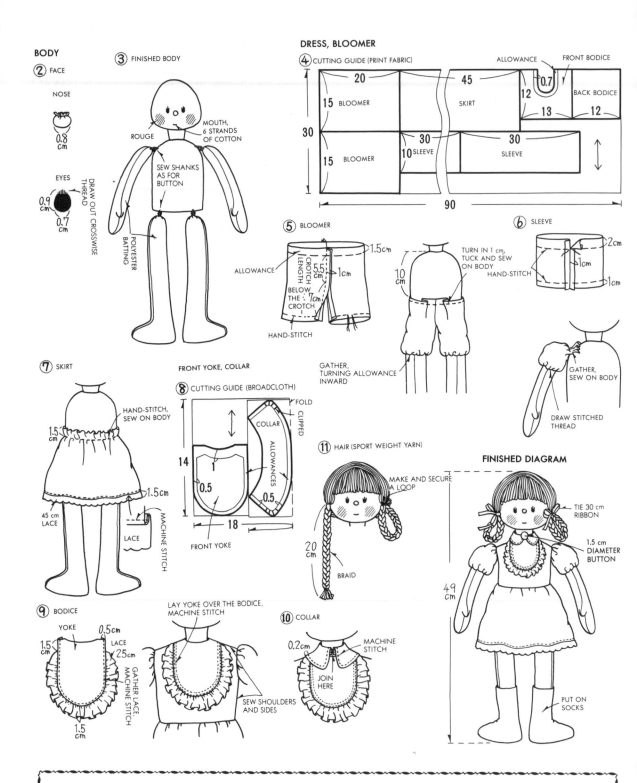

BODY

② FACE

③ FINISHED BODY

NOSE

0.8 cm

EYES

0.9 cm

0.7 cm

DRAW OUT CROSSWISE THREAD

ROUGE

MOUTH, 6 STRANDS OF COTTON

SEW SHANKS AS FOR BUTTON

POLYESTER BATTING

DRESS, BLOOMER

④ CUTTING GUIDE (PRINT FABRIC)

ALLOWANCE

FRONT BODICE

0.7

20

15 BLOOMER

45

SKIRT

12

BACK BODICE

13

12

30

15 BLOOMER

30

10 SLEEVE

30

SLEEVE

90

⑤ BLOOMER

1.5 cm

ALLOWANCE

CROTCH LENGTH

5.5 cm

1 cm

BELOW THE CROTCH

7 cm

HAND-STITCH

TURN IN 1 cm, TUCK AND SEW ON BODY

10 cm

HAND-STITCH

GATHER, TURNING ALLOWANCE INWARD

⑥ SLEEVE

2 cm

1 cm

1 cm

GATHER, SEW ON BODY

DRAW STITCHED THREAD

⑦ SKIRT

HAND-STITCH, SEW ON BODY

1.5 cm

1.5 cm

45 cm LACE

LACE

MACHINE STITCH

FRONT YOKE, COLLAR

⑧ CUTTING GUIDE (BROADCLOTH)

FOLD

COLLAR

CLIPPED

ALLOWANCES

14

1

0.5

0.5

18

FRONT YOKE

⑪ HAIR (SPORT WEIGHT YARN)

MAKE AND SECURE A LOOP

20 cm

BRAID

FINISHED DIAGRAM

TIE 30 cm RIBBON

1.5 cm DIAMETER BUTTON

49 cm

PUT ON SOCKS

⑨ BODICE

YOKE

0.5 cm

1.5 cm

LACE

25 cm

GATHER LACE, MACHINE STITCH

1.5 cm

LAY YOKE OVER THE BODICE, MACHINE STITCH

SEW SHOULDERS AND SIDES

⑩ COLLAR

0.2 cm

MACHINE STITCH

JOIN HERE

SHIGERU & CHIKO

Shown on page 15.

Use new-born baby socks. Sweater and muffler are paired like those of a modern young couple.

YOU'LL NEED (body materials are for both):
Head-Foundation, Body, Arms, Legs—73 cm by 48 cm white rayon. Face, Nose, Arms, Legs—63 cm by 48 cm beige cotton jersey. Eyes—dacron georgette. Mouth— strands of embroidery thread. Hair—sport-weight yarn, 40 cm of 0.6 cm ribbon. Also—New-born baby socks, packing, cotton wadding, polyester batting.

(Shigeru): Sweater—lighweight yarn. Pants—36 cm by 12 cm wool fabric.

(Chiko): Blouse—70 cm by 16 cm white jersey, 23 cm of 1 cm braid. Bloomer—36 cm by 12 cm white rayon. Jumper Skirt—20 cm by 23.5 cm felt, strands of embroidery cotton, Two 1.5 cm diameter buttons.

FINISHED SIZE: Refer to diagram.

INSTRUCTIONS;

The basic method is the same as for Hiji, so refer to pages 50-64.

(Shigeru): Make head beforehand, and set in position by making a hole on the body after sweater is on. Sew on hair as shown on page 72.

(Chiko): Make the body in same way as for Shigeru. Part the yarn for hair in half, sew on in same manner as Hiji's, as shown. Knit muffler, wrap round the neck.

① PATTERNS (ACTUAL SIZE):

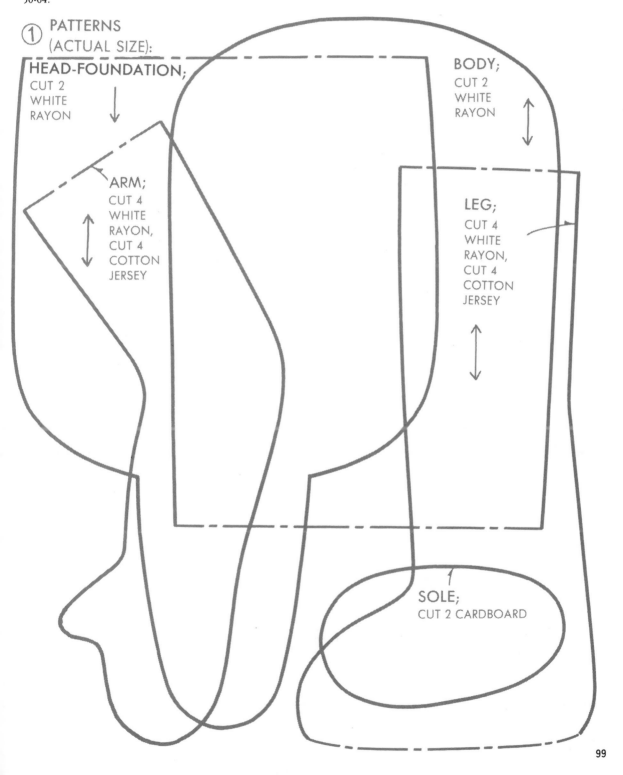

HEAD-FOUNDATION;
CUT 2
WHITE
RAYON

BODY;
CUT 2
WHITE
RAYON

ARM;
CUT 4
WHITE
RAYON,
CUT 4
COTTON
JERSEY

LEG;
CUT 4
WHITE
RAYON,
CUT 4
COTTON
JERSEY

SOLE;
CUT 2 CARDBOARD

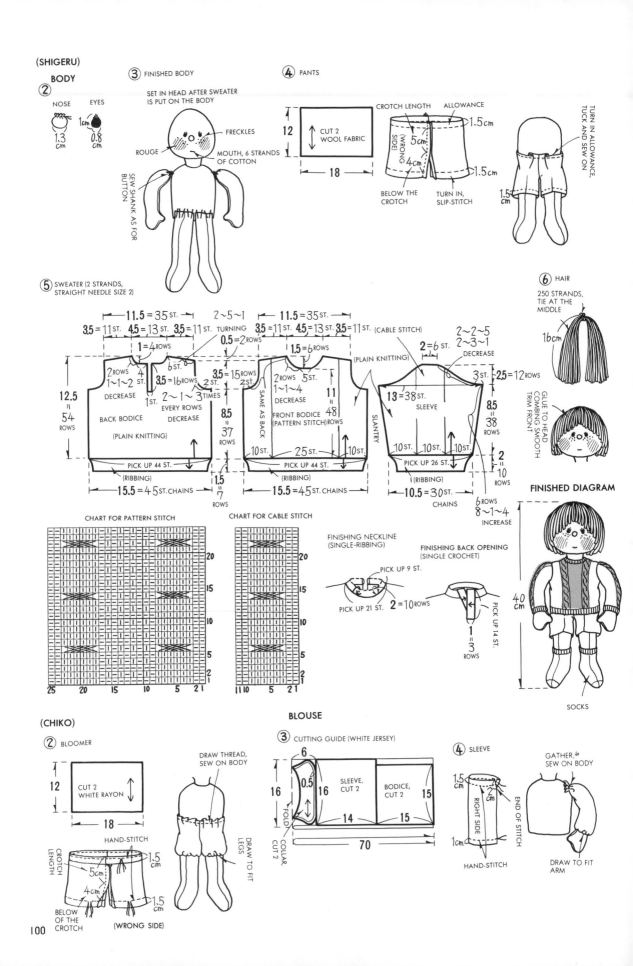

(SHIGERU)

BODY

② NOSE 1.3 cm EYES 1 cm 0.8 cm

③ FINISHED BODY

SET IN HEAD AFTER SWEATER IS PUT ON THE BODY

FRECKLES
ROUGE
MOUTH, 6 STRANDS OF COTTON
SEW SHANK AS FOR BUTTON

④ PANTS

12 CUT 2 WOOL FABRIC 18

CROTCH LENGTH   ALLOWANCE
1.5 cm
(WRONG SIDE) 5 cm 4 cm
1.5 cm
BELOW THE CROTCH   TURN IN, SLIP-STITCH

TURN IN ALLOWANCE, TUCK AND SEW ON
1.5 cm

⑤ SWEATER (2 STRANDS, STRAIGHT NEEDLE SIZE 2)

⑥ HAIR
250 STRANDS, TIE AT THE MIDDLE
16 cm

GLUE TO HEAD COMBING SMOOTH TRIM FRONT

— 11.5 = 35 ST. —   2~5~1   — 11.5 = 35 ST. —   (CABLE STITCH)
3.5 = 11 ST. 4.5 = 13 ST. 3.5 = 11 ST. TURNING   3.5 = 11 ST. 4.5 = 13 ST. 3.5 = 11 ST. (PLAIN KNITTING)
2~2~5 2~3~1 DECREASE
1 = 4 ROWS   0.5 = 2 ROWS   1.5 = 6 ROWS   2 = 6 ST.
2 ROWS 4 ST.   6 ST.   3.5 = 16 ROWS   3.5 = 15 ROWS 2 ST.   2 ROWS 5 ST.   11   3 ST.   2.5 = 12 ROWS
1~1~2   1 ST.   2~1~3 TIMES   1~1~4 DECREASE   48   13 = 38 ST. SLEEVE   8.5 = 38 ROWS
12.5 = 54 ROWS   DECREASE   EVERY ROWS DECREASE   8.5 = 37 ROWS   SAME AS BACK   FRONT BODICE (PATTERN STITCH)   SLANTRY
BACK BODICE (PLAIN KNITTING)
PICK UP 44 ST.   10 ST.   25 ST.   10 ST.   10 ST.   10 ST.   10 ST.   2 = 10 ROWS
(RIBBING)   1.5 = 7 ROWS   PICK UP 44 ST. (RIBBING)   PICK UP 26 ST. (RIBBING)
— 15.5 = 45 ST. CHAINS —   — 15.5 = 45 ST. CHAINS —   — 10.5 = 30 ST. CHAINS —
6 ROWS 8~1~4 INCREASE

CHART FOR PATTERN STITCH

20 / 15 / 10 / 5 / 2 / 1
25 20 15 10 5 2 1

CHART FOR CABLE STITCH

20 / 15 / 10 / 5 / 2 / 1
11 10 5 2 1

FINISHING NECKLINE (SINGLE-RIBBING)
PICK UP 9 ST.
PICK UP 21 ST.   2 = 10 ROWS

FINISHING BACK OPENING (SINGLE CROCHET)
1 = 3 ROWS   PICK UP 14 ST.

FINISHED DIAGRAM
40 cm
SOCKS

(CHIKO)

② BLOOMER

12 CUT 2 WHITE RAYON 18

DRAW THREAD, SEW ON BODY

HAND-STITCH
CROTCH LENGTH 5 cm 4 cm   1.5 cm   1.5 cm
BELOW OF THE CROTCH   (WRONG SIDE)
DRAW TO FIT LEGS

BLOUSE

③ CUTTING GUIDE (WHITE JERSEY)

6   0.5   16
16   SLEEVE, CUT 2   BODICE, CUT 2   15
FOLD, CUT 2   14   15
COLLAR, CUT 2   70

④ SLEEVE

1.5 cm   RIGHT SIDE   2 cm   1 cm
HAND-STITCH   END OF STITCH
GATHER, SEW ON BODY   DRAW TO FIT ARM

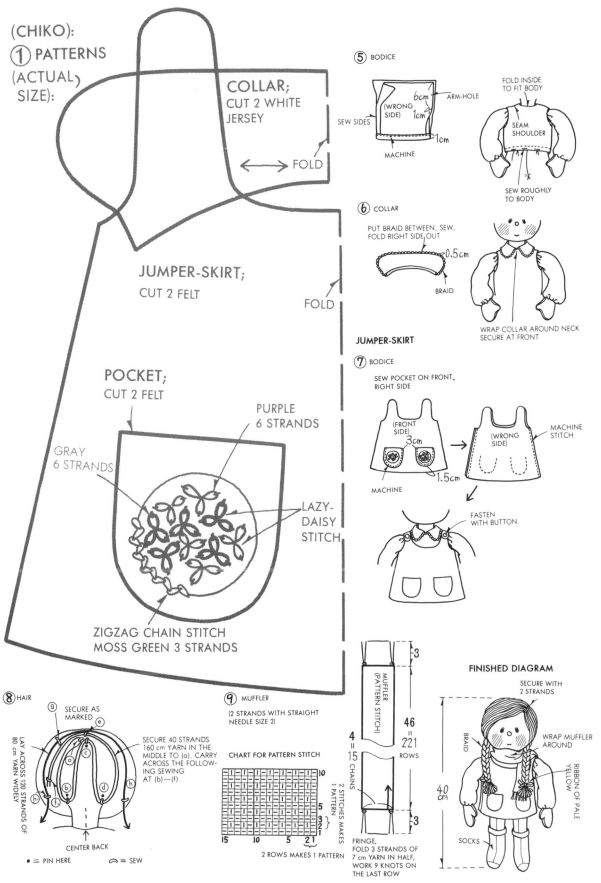

(CHIKO):
① PATTERNS (ACTUAL SIZE):

COLLAR;
CUT 2 WHITE JERSEY

← FOLD →

JUMPER-SKIRT;
CUT 2 FELT

FOLD

POCKET;
CUT 2 FELT

PURPLE 6 STRANDS

GRAY 6 STRANDS

LAZY-DAISY STITCH

ZIGZAG CHAIN STITCH
MOSS GREEN 3 STRANDS

⑤ BODICE

6cm
(WRONG SIDE)
ARM-HOLE
1cm
SEW SIDES
MACHINE
1cm

FOLD INSIDE TO FIT BODY
SEAM SHOULDER
SEW ROUGHLY TO BODY

⑥ COLLAR

PUT BRAID BETWEEN, SEW, FOLD RIGHT SIDE OUT
0.5cm
BRAID

WRAP COLLAR AROUND NECK SECURE AT FRONT

JUMPER-SKIRT

⑦ BODICE

SEW POCKET ON FRONT, RIGHT SIDE

(FRONT SIDE)
3cm
MACHINE
1.5cm

(WRONG SIDE)
MACHINE STITCH

FASTEN WITH BUTTON

⑧ HAIR

SECURE AS MARKED

LAY ACROSS 120 STRANDS OF 80 cm YARN WIDELY

SECURE 40 STRANDS 160 cm YARN IN THE MIDDLE TO (a), CARRY ACROSS THE FOLLOWING SEWING AT (b)—(f)

CENTER BACK

● = PIN HERE   ⌢ = SEW

⑨ MUFFLER

(2 STRANDS WITH STRAIGHT NEEDLE SIZE 2)

CHART FOR PATTERN STITCH

10

5

3
2
1

15   10   5   2 1

2 ROWS MAKES 1 PATTERN

2 STITCHES MAKES 1 PATTERN

MUFFLER (PATTERN STITCH)

3

46
"
221
ROWS

4
=
15
CHAINS

3

FRINGE, FOLD 3 STRANDS OF 7 cm YARN IN HALF, WORK 9 KNOTS ON THE LAST ROW

FINISHED DIAGRAM

SECURE WITH 2 STRANDS

BRAID

WRAP MUFFLER AROUND

RIBBON OF PALE YELLOW

40 cm

SOCKS

101

AKKO & GORO & KENTA

Shown on pages 16–17.

Stain their clothes with gray powder eye-shadow. The three are from one pattern, and the boys clothes are made the same way. These playmates with mischievous faces have been in the dirt!

YOU'LL NEED (body materials are for the set):
Head-Foundation, Body, Arms, Legs—70 cm by 38 cm white rayon. Face, Nose, Arms, Legs—55 cm by 25 cm cotton jersey. Eyes—dacron georgette. Mouth—strands of embroidery thread. Hair—lightweight yarn, 40 cm of 0.6 cm ribbon. Also—packing, cotton wadding, polyester batting.
(Akko): Dress, Bloomer—58 cm by 29 cm cotton print. Adhesive plaster—white cotton fabric.
(Goro): Shirt—50 cm by 14 cm cotton print. Overalls—56 cm by 18 cm lightweight denim, strands of embroidery cotton.

(Kenta): Shirt—50 cm by 14 cm striped cotton. Overalls—56 cm by 18 cm lightweight denim, strands of embroidery cotton.
FINISHED SIZE: Refer to diagram.
INSTRUCTIONS:
Make three bodies in the same way, referring to pages 50-64 for basic directions.
Akk: Cut out dress and bloomers as shown and put on body. Sew on hair in same manner as for Hiji, making a braid and ribbon loop on each side.
Goro: Cut out shirt and overall as shown and put on body. Sew on hair (refer to page 72).
Kenta: Make in same manner as for Goro.

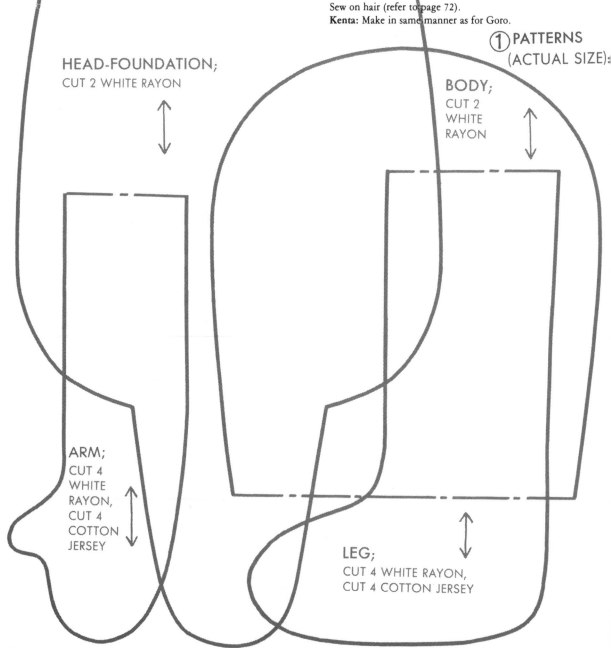

① PATTERNS (ACTUAL SIZE):

HEAD-FOUNDATION; CUT 2 WHITE RAYON

BODY; CUT 2 WHITE RAYON

ARM; CUT 4 WHITE RAYON, CUT 4 COTTON JERSEY

LEG; CUT 4 WHITE RAYON, CUT 4 COTTON JERSEY

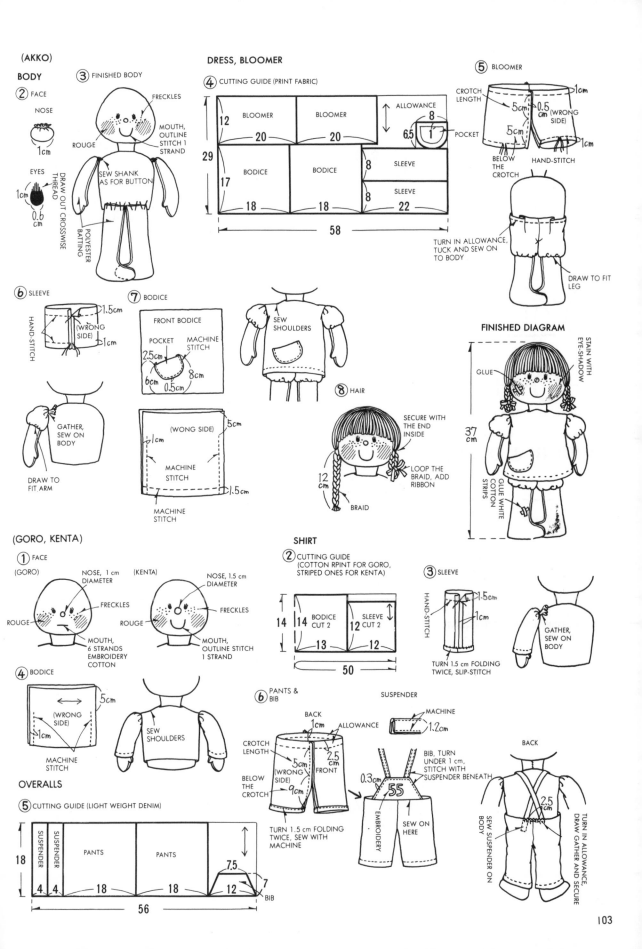

(AKKO)

BODY

② FACE

NOSE

1cm

EYES

1cm
0.6 cm

DRAW OUT CROSSWISE THREAD

③ FINISHED BODY

FRECKLES

ROUGE

MOUTH, OUTLINE STITCH 1 STRAND

SEW SHANK AS FOR BUTTON

POLYESTER BATTING

DRESS, BLOOMER

④ CUTTING GUIDE (PRINT FABRIC)

12	BLOOMER 20	BLOOMER 20	ALLOWANCE
29 / 17	BODICE 18	BODICE 18	SLEEVE 8 / SLEEVE 8 / 22

8 / 6.5 / 1 POCKET

58

⑤ BLOOMER

CROTCH LENGTH

5cm / 0.5cm (WRONG SIDE) / 1cm

5cm

BELOW THE CROTCH / HAND-STITCH / 1cm

TURN IN ALLOWANCE, TUCK AND SEW ON TO BODY

DRAW TO FIT LEG

⑥ SLEEVE

1.5cm / (WRONG SIDE) / 1cm

HAND-STITCH

GATHER, SEW ON BODY

DRAW TO FIT ARM

⑦ BODICE

FRONT BODICE

POCKET / MACHINE STITCH

2.5cm / 8cm / 6cm / 0.5cm

(WONG SIDE)

1cm / 5cm

MACHINE STITCH / 1.5cm

MACHINE STITCH

SEW SHOULDERS

⑧ HAIR

SECURE WITH THE END INSIDE

LOOP THE BRAID, ADD RIBBON

12 cm

BRAID

FINISHED DIAGRAM

STAIN WITH EYE-SHADOW

GLUE

37 cm

GLUE WHITE COTTON STRIPS

(GORO, KENTA)

① FACE

(GORO)

NOSE, 1 cm DIAMETER

FRECKLES

ROUGE

MOUTH, 6 STRANDS EMBROIDERY COTTON

(KENTA)

NOSE, 1.5 cm DIAMETER

FRECKLES

ROUGE

MOUTH, OUTLINE STITCH 1 STRAND

④ BODICE

5cm / (WRONG SIDE) / 1cm

MACHINE STITCH

SEW SHOULDERS

OVERALLS

⑤ CUTTING GUIDE (LIGHT WEIGHT DENIM)

18	SUSPENDER / SUSPENDER	PANTS	PANTS	7.5 / 12 / 7	
	4 / 4	18	18	BIB	

56

SHIRT

② CUTTING GUIDE (COTTON RPINT FOR GORO, STRIPED ONES FOR KENTA)

14	14 / BODICE Cut 2 / 13	12 / SLEEVE Cut 2 / 12

50

③ SLEEVE

1.5cm / 1cm

HAND-STITCH

TURN 1.5 cm FOLDING TWICE, SLIP-STITCH

GATHER, SEW ON BODY

⑥ PANTS & BIB

BACK

1cm / ALLOWANCE

CROTCH LENGTH

5cm / (WRONG SIDE) / 9cm

2.5 cm FRONT

BELOW THE CROTCH

TURN 1.5 cm FOLDING TWICE, SEW WITH MACHINE

SUSPENDER

MACHINE / 1.2cm

0.3cm

BIB, TURN UNDER 1 cm, STITCH WITH SUSPENDER BENEATH

55 / EMBROIDERY / SEW ON HERE

BACK

2.5 cm

SEW SUSPENDER ON BODY

TURN IN ALLOWANCE, DRAW GATHER AND SECURE

CHAIN STITCH

(GORO)

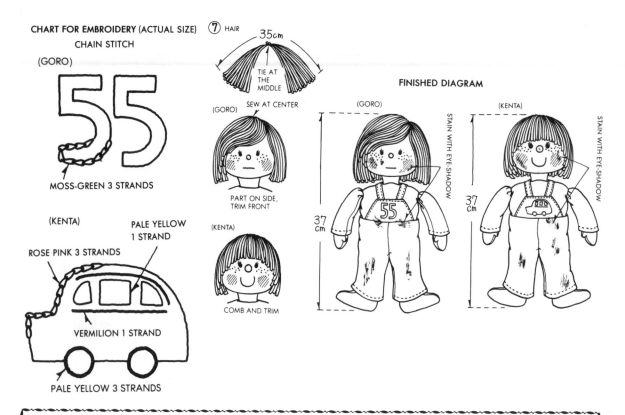

MOSS-GREEN 3 STRANDS

(KENTA)

PALE YELLOW 1 STRAND

ROSE PINK 3 STRANDS

VERMILION 1 STRAND

PALE YELLOW 3 STRANDS

⑦ HAIR

35cm

TIE AT THE MIDDLE

(GORO) SEW AT CENTER

PART ON SIDE, TRIM FRONT

(KENTA)

COMB AND TRIM

FINISHED DIAGRAM

(GORO)

STAIN WITH EYE-SHADOW

37 cm

(KENTA)

STAIN WITH EYE-SHADOW

37 Cm

MIDORI & OYUKI

Shown on pages 18-19.

Both are made from the same pattern. Create hair styles by combing neatly, and try to use traditional Japanese fabrics.

YOU'LL NEED (for each):

Head-Foundation, Body, Arms, Legs—72 cm by 50 cm white rayon. Face, Nose, Arms, Legs—60 cm by 50 cm cotton jersey. Eyes—dacron georgette. Mouth—strands of embroidery thread. Hair—sport-weight yarn, worsted-weight yarn, 14 cm by 15 cm broadcloth, artificial flowers. Kimono—86 cm by 72 cm cotton fabric. Belt—90 cm by 15 cm broadcloth. Collar—8 cm by 25 cm broadcloth. Also—packing, cotton wadding, polyester batting.

FINISHED SIZE: Refer to diagram.

INSTRUCTIONS:

The basic method is the same as for Hiji, so refer to pages 50-64.

Sew arms on body, setting in properly; then assemble kimono.

Sew collar on body first; make bodice and put on, securing lower half of the front. Make and put on bottom part of kimono. Sew belt, put round the waist hiding all the allowances benath, tie on back.

Sew on hair in same manner as for Hiji, bundle as shown, wrap with fabric piece and secure, putting flowers and decorative band together.

BODY

② FACE

NOSE   EYES

③ FINISHED BODY

ROUGE

MOUTH, 6 STRANDS OF COTTON

1cm   DRAW OUT CROSSWISE THREAD

1cm   0.8cm

SEW ON

POLYESTER BATTING

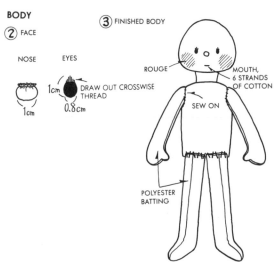

KIMONO

④ COLLAR (BROADCLOTH)

8

FOLD HERE

25

SEW ON COLLAR ROUGHLY

LAY WADDING THINLY

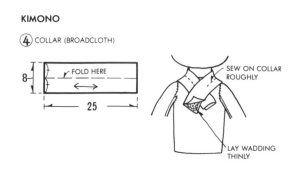

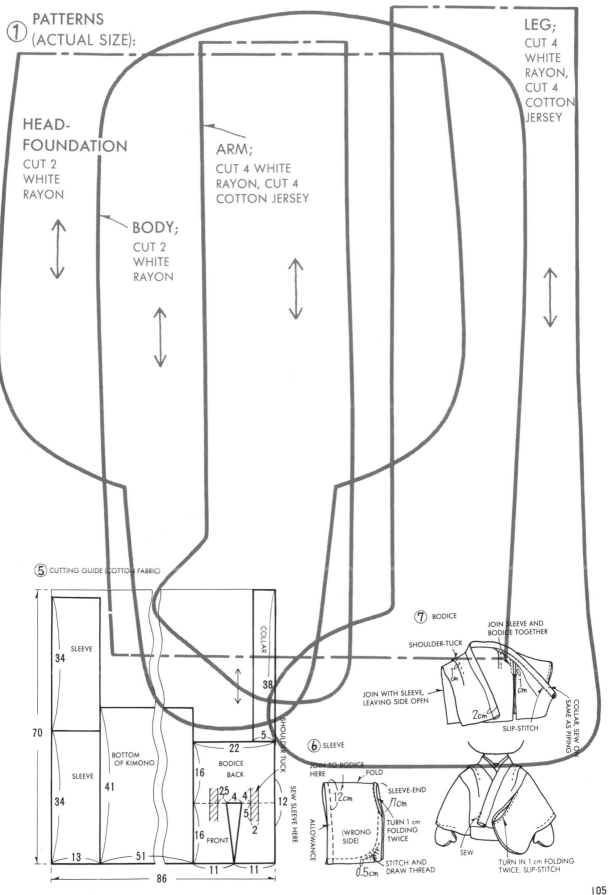

① PATTERNS
(ACTUAL SIZE):

HEAD-
FOUNDATION
CUT 2
WHITE
RAYON

BODY;
CUT 2
WHITE
RAYON

ARM;
CUT 4 WHITE
RAYON, CUT 4
COTTON JERSEY

LEG;
CUT 4
WHITE
RAYON,
CUT 4
COTTON
JERSEY

⑤ Cutting Guide (COTTON FABRIC)

SLEEVE 34

SLEEVE 34

70

BOTTOM
OF KIMONO
41

13

51

86

COLLAR

38

5

22

16

16 FRONT

BODICE
BACK

25 4 4
5
2

SHOULDER TUCK

SEW SLEEVE HERE

12

11   11

⑦ BODICE

SHOULDER-TUCK

JOIN SLEEVE AND
BODICE TOGETHER

JOIN WITH SLEEVE,
LEAVING SIDE OPEN

1
cm

1
cm

2cm

SLIP-STITCH

COLLAR, SEW ON
SAME AS PIPING

⑥ SLEEVE

JOIN TO BODICE
HERE

FOLD

SLEEVE-END

1cm

12cm

ALLOWANCE

(WRONG
SIDE)

TURN 1 cm
FOLDING
TWICE

STITCH AND
DRAW THREAD

0.5cm

SEW

TURN IN 1 cm FOLDING
TWICE, SLIP-STITCH

105

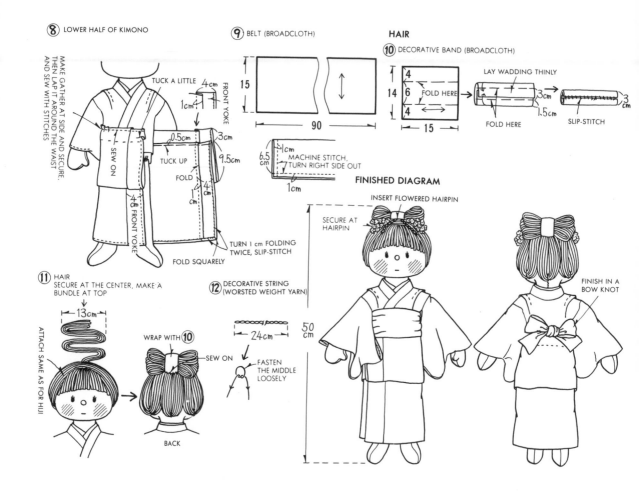

PRINCE & PRINCESS

Shown on pages 20-21.

Put a piece of wire into their arms and legs and pose them as you like. Make a stand of board 2.5 cm or higher, and make a hole with a gimlet to set each foot firmly on the board.

YOU'LL NEED (body materials for both):

Head-Foundation, Body, Arms, Legs—50 cm by 30 cm white rayon. Face, Nose, Arms—33 cm by 28 cm beige georgette. Eyes—dacron georgette. Mouth—strands of embroidery thread. Hair—mohair yarn. Also—wire No. 12, No. 18, packing, cotton wadding, polyester batting.

(Prince): Legs-28 cm by 14 cm silver lamé. Sleeves—24 cm by 16 cm dacron seersucker, 40 cm of 2 cm lace. Bodice, Hat—44 cm by 13 cm purple felt, 100 cm of 2.5 cm braid. Shoes—26 cm of 2 cm black and gold braid, 5 cm by 4.5 cm black felt.

(Princess): Legs, Bloomers—28 cm by 26 cm white georgette, 44 cm of 4 cm lace. Petticoat—40 cm by 11 cm non-woven fabric. Dress—64 cm by 20 cm white lace, 170 cm of 1.8 cm floral braid. 15 cm of 2 cm lace. Hair Ornament, Bouquet—artificial flowers, leaves. 10 cm of 1.8 cm floral braid. Shoes—26 cm of 2 cm pale pink braid. 5 cm by 4.5 cm white felt.

FINISHED SIZE: Refer to diagram.
INSTRUCTIONS:

The basic method is the same as for Hiji, so refer to pages 50-64.

Prince: Make arms and legs with wire inserted in the middle, and connect it with wire inserted into the body.

Make him stand by connecting the wires from the legs to his stand.

Princess: Make body in same manner as for prince, put on underwear and dress.

Sew on hair in the same way as for Hiji, attach back hair of twined yarns. Sew on hair ornament, and let her hold bouquet in the bent hand.

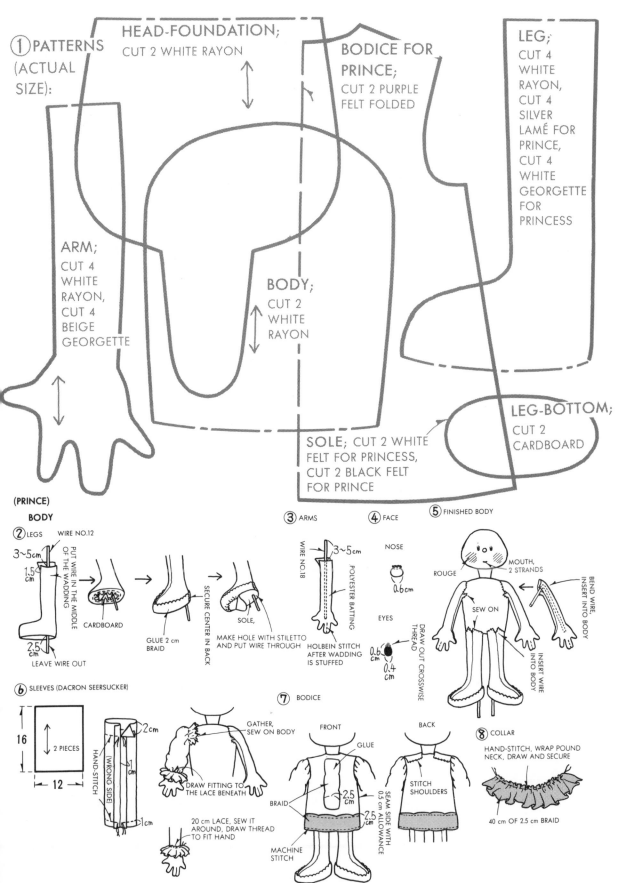

① PATTERNS (ACTUAL SIZE):

HEAD-FOUNDATION; CUT 2 WHITE RAYON

BODICE FOR PRINCE; CUT 2 PURPLE FELT FOLDED

LEG; CUT 4 WHITE RAYON, CUT 4 SILVER LAMÉ FOR PRINCE, CUT 4 WHITE GEORGETTE FOR PRINCESS

ARM; CUT 4 WHITE RAYON, CUT 4 BEIGE GEORGETTE

BODY; CUT 2 WHITE RAYON

LEG-BOTTOM; CUT 2 CARDBOARD

SOLE; CUT 2 WHITE FELT FOR PRINCESS, CUT 2 BLACK FELT FOR PRINCE

(PRINCE) BODY

② LEGS   WIRE NO.12

3~5cm

1.5cm

PUT WIRE IN THE MIDDLE OF THE WADDING

CARDBOARD

GLUE 2 cm BRAID

SECURE CENTER IN BACK

SOLE,

MAKE HOLE WITH STILETTO AND PUT WIRE THROUGH

2.5cm

LEAVE WIRE OUT

③ ARMS

WIRE NO.18

3~5cm

POLYESTER BATTING

HOLBEIN STITCH AFTER WADDING IS STUFFED

④ FACE

NOSE

0.6cm

EYES

0.6cm   0.4cm

DRAW OUT CROSSWISE THREAD

⑤ FINISHED BODY

ROUGE

MOUTH, 2 STRANDS

SEW ON

BEND WIRE, INSERT INTO BODY

INSERT WIRE INTO BODY

⑥ SLEEVES (DACRON SEERSUCKER)

16

2 PIECES

12

HAND-STITCH

(WRONG SIDE)

2cm

1cm

1cm

GATHER, SEW ON BODY

DRAW FITTING TO THE LACE BENEATH

20 cm LACE, SEW IT AROUND, DRAW THREAD TO FIT HAND

⑦ BODICE

FRONT

GLUE

BRAID

MACHINE STITCH

2.5cm

2.5cm

BACK

STITCH SHOULDERS

SEAM SIDE WITH 0.5 cm ALLOWANCE

⑧ COLLAR

HAND-STITCH, WRAP POUND NECK, DRAW AND SECURE

40 cm OF 2.5 cm BRAID

⑨ HAIR

WIND 100 TIMES

40 cm

PUT YARN ACROSS AND FASTEN

GLUE HAIR AFTER COMBING NEATLY

BACK

⑩ HAT

10 10

10

20

CLIP

0.3cm

MACHINE

ORNAMENT

30 cm OF 2.5 cm BRAID

INSERT WIRE INTO BRAID, BEND BOTH ENDS

BRAID

FINISHED DIAGRAM

ORNAMENT

COLLAR

29 cm

APPLY GLUE INSIDE SET ON HEAD

ATTACH ORNAMENT

WIRE

(PRINCESS)

UNDERWEAR

① SHOES

PALE PINK BRAID

SHOE-SOLE

② BLOOMER

12

14

CUT 2 WHITE GEORGETTE

22 cm LONG LACE

DRAW THREAD TO FIT THE LEG

1cm

3cm

1.5 cm

4.5 cm

(WRONG SIDE)

CROTCH LENGTH

HAND-STITCH

5cm

1cm

BELOW THE CROTCH

SEW ON BODY

GATHER TO FIT THE LACE BELOW

BACK

TUCK ON

③ PETTICOAT

11

40

CUT 1 NON-WOVEN FABRIC

DRAW TO FIT ON THE BODY

0.5 cm

FINISH HEM IN A SCALLOPED CUT

DRESS

④ CUTTING GUIDE (LACE FABRIC)

20

10   10

SLEEVE

3 8

10 10

14

SLEEVE

3

BODICE

14   10

SKIRT

40

64

⑤ SLEEVE

2cm

HAND-STITCH

1 cm

1cm

MACHINE STITCH

1.5cm

GLUE BRAID

GATHER, SEW ON BODY

⑥ SKIRT

ALLOWANCE

1cm 1cm

HAND-STITCH

STITCH INTO ROUND

1cm

2.5cm

CENTER BACK

MACHINE STITCH BRAID

1cm

CENTER FRONT

FINISH HEM WITH CARE NOT TO OVERSTITCH

PUT ON BODY AND GATHER

1cm

⑦ BODICE

LAY POLYESTER BATTING THINLY ON THE BODY UNDER BODICE

GLUE BRAID (BACK SIDE ALSO)

ATTACH 1 PATTERN OUT OF THE BRAID

⑧ COLLAR

HAND-STITCH DRAW TO FIT NECK, SECURE

15 cm OF 2 cm LACE

FINISHED DIAGRAM

ATTACH FLOWERS ON THE FLOWER-BRAID

ARTIFICIAL FLOWERS

25 cm

⑨ HAIR

FASTEN TO (9)

TWINE THE FOLDED TOGETHER

70 cm

TWINE, FOLD IN HALF

SEWING AT THE BACK HAIR

(h)

(g)

FOLD

REFER TO (PAGE64) UP TO (g)
SECURE TWINED YARNS TOGETHER AT (9), PART THEM IN HALF, SECURE THE FOLLOWING AS SHOWN

FRONT

SECURE

MAKE FRONT HAIR ROUND

BACK

FOLD

THE WOOD ELVES

Shown on page 22.

The arms and legs of these very simple dolls move freely. If strings were tied to them, they would become marionettes. Emphasize the humorous expressions in their features.

YOU'LL NEED (for each):
Head-Foundation, Body, Arms, Legs—40 cm by 30 cm white rayon. Face, Arms—70 cm by 22 cm beige cotton jersey. Legs—35 cm by 14 cm striped cotton. Nose—scrap of orange jersey. Eyes—dacron georgette. Mouth—strands of embroidery thread. Hair—heavyweight yarn. Clothes—30 cm by 29 cm olive green felt, 2 of 1.2 cm diameter button. Shoes—16 cm by 8 cm pale yellow felt. Also—packing, cotton wadding, polyester batting.
FINISHED SIZE: Refer to diagram.

INSTRUCTIONS:
The basic method is the same as for Hiji, so refer to pages 50-64.
Make legs with striped fabric, finished in the same way as arms. Color nose fabric with a felttip pen. Sew on hair as shown on page 72, finish front hair in a ladder cut.

① PATTERNS (ACTUAL SIZE):

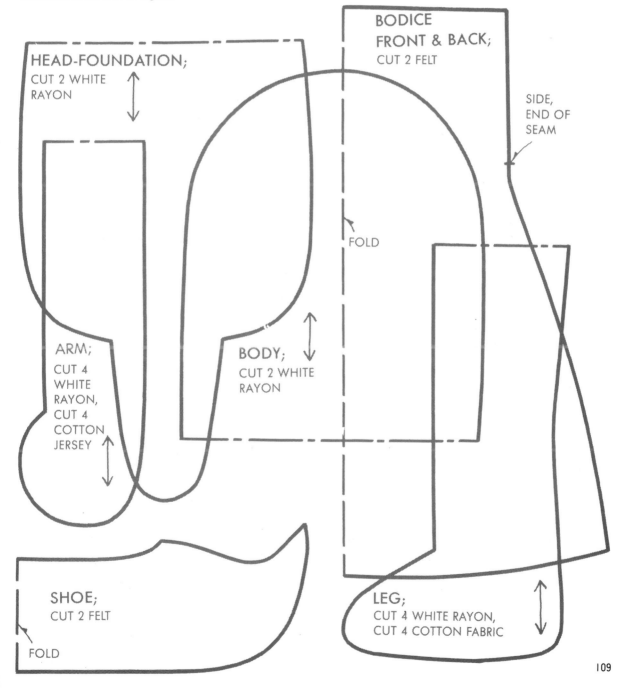

HEAD-FOUNDATION;
CUT 2 WHITE RAYON

BODICE FRONT & BACK;
CUT 2 FELT

SIDE, END OF SEAM

FOLD

ARM;
CUT 4 WHITE RAYON, CUT 4 COTTON JERSEY

BODY;
CUT 2 WHITE RAYON

SHOE;
CUT 2 FELT

FOLD

LEG;
CUT 4 WHITE RAYON, CUT 4 COTTON FABRIC

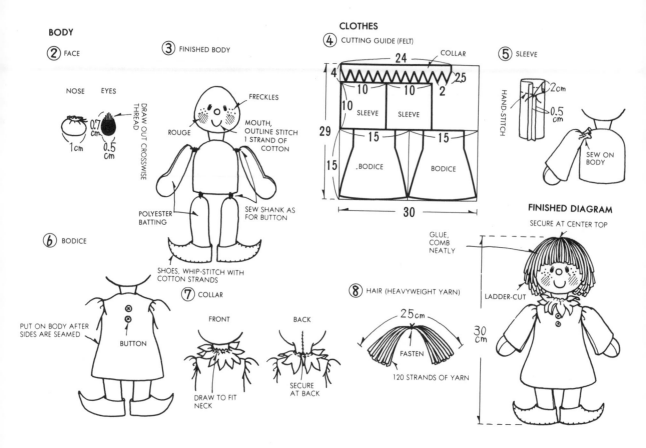

BODY

② FACE

NOSE EYES

0.7 cm

1cm 0.5 cm

DRAW OUT CROSSWISE THREAD

③ FINISHED BODY

FRECKLES

MOUTH, OUTLINE STITCH 1 STRAND OF COTTON

ROUGE

POLYESTER BATTING

SEW SHANK AS FOR BUTTON

SHOES, WHIP-STITCH WITH COTTON STRANDS

⑥ BODICE

PUT ON BODY AFTER SIDES ARE SEAMED

BUTTON

⑦ COLLAR

FRONT

BACK

DRAW TO FIT NECK

SECURE AT BACK

CLOTHES

④ CUTTING GUIDE (FELT)

COLLAR

24

4 25

10 10 2

10 SLEEVE SLEEVE

29 15 15

15 BODICE BODICE

30

⑤ SLEEVE

2cm

HAND-STITCH

0.5 cm

SEW ON BODY

FINISHED DIAGRAM

SECURE AT CENTER TOP

GLUE, COMB NEATLY

LADDER-CUT

30 cm

⑧ HAIR (HEAVYWEIGHT YARN)

25cm

FASTEN

120 STRANDS OF YARN

LOST ANGELS

Shown on page 23.

Arms and legs are finished with wire inside, so pose them as you like. The hair ornament used here is a braid of flowers that you may make.

YOU'LL NEED (for each):
Head-Foundation, Body, Arms, Legs—48 cm by 30 cm white rayon. Face, Nose, Arms, Legs—64 cm by 16 cm cotton jersey. Eyes—dacron georgette. Mouth—strands of embroidery thread. Hair—Lightweight yarn, 20 cm of 1.2 cm floral braid. Clothes—46 cm by 10.5 wool georgette. Wings—13 cm by 6.5 cm white lace fabric, non-woven iron-on interfacing. Also—No. 18 wire, packing, cotton wadding, polyester batting.
FINISHED SIZE: Refer to diagram.

INSTRUCTIONS:
The basic method is the same as for Hiji, so refer to pages 50-64.
Stuff polyester batting into top parts of arms and legs only, insert the wire wrapped with wadding right into the middle. Sew on legs in a sitting position.
Attach the wings of lace fabric pressed with non-woven fabric on back.
Bend hands to make them pose.

BODY

② ARMS, LEGS

3~5cm

THICK

1cm

LEG

LEAVE OPEN

1cm ARM

WRAP WADDING ROUND WIRE

MAKE THINNER

STUFF TOP ONLY

STUFF TOP ONLY

POLYESTER BATTING

③ FACE

NOSE EYES

0.5cm

0.4 cm

0.6 cm

DRAW OUT CROSSWISE THREAD

ATTACH OBLIQUELY

ROUGE

MOUTH, OUTLINE STITCH 1 STRAND

④ FINISHED BODY

BEND WIRE, INSERT INTO SHOULDER, SLIP-STITCH

SEW ON IN SITTING POSITION

BEND WIRE, INSERT INTO BODY

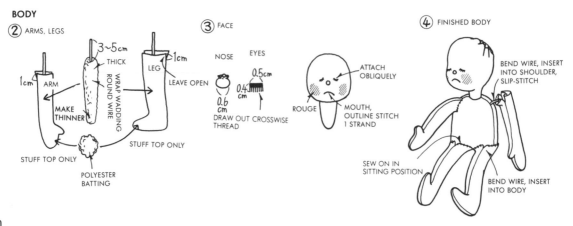

① PATTERNS (ACTUAL SIZE):

ARM;
CUT 4
WHITE
RAYON,
CUT 4
COTTON
JERSEY

HEAD-
FOUNDATION;
CUT 2 WHITE
RAYON

BODY;
CUT 2
WHITE
RAYON

LEG;
CUT 4
WHITE
RAYON,
CUT 4
COTTON
JERSEY

WING;
CUT 1 EACH,
WHITE LACE FABRIC,
NON-WOVEN FABRIC,
FOLDED

FOLD

GLUE ON BACK

CLOTHES

⑤ CUTTING GUIDE (GEORGETTE)

10.5

BODICE	BODICE	PANTS
13	13	8	20

46

⑥ PANTS

ALLOWANCE
1cm

1cm

HAND-STITCH

TURN IN
ALLOWANCE

PUT ON BODY, DRAW TO
FIT LEGS,
SEW CROTCH

⑦ BLOUSE

BODICE
(WRONG
SIDE)
1cm
ARM-HOLE
3.5cm
TURN 2 cm
FOLDING TWICE,
SLIP-STITCH
SIDE,
SEAM
5 cm

PUT ON BODY,
SEW SHOULDERS

⑧ HAIR (LIGHTWEIGHT YARN)

WIND 35 TIMES

FASTEN

SEW ON ALL OVER
HEAD

⑨ FLORAL
BRAID

GLUE INTO
CIRCLE

BACK

BODY
TUCK, SEW
ON BODY

FINISHED DIAGRAM

ORNAMENT,
GLUE TO HAIR

WING,
GLUE ON CENTER
BACK

BEND
ARM

16
cm

BEND AT
WRIST

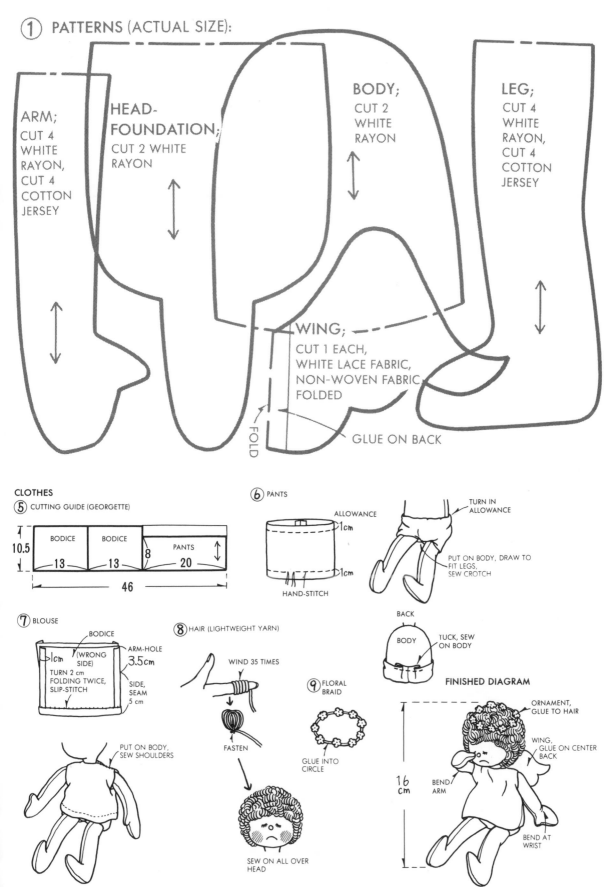

111

FANTASY

Shown on pages 24-25.

Those are posed dolls, clothed in felt. Make silver flute, wrapping tin foil over a piece of wire. Use same pattern for all fairies. Note the girl's lovely mood.

YOU'LL NEED:

(Each Boy): Head-Foundation, Body—40 cm by 13 cm white rayon. Face, Nose—12 cm by 14 cm cotton jersey. Arms, Legs—48 cm by 12 cm striped cotton. Eyes—dacron georgette. Mouth—strands of embroidery thread. Hair—mohair yarn. Clothes—38 cm by 12.5 cm green felt, 20 cm of 1.3 cm braid. Also—No. 18 wire, packing, cotton wadding, polyester batting.

(Girl): Head-Foundation, Body, Arms, Legs—88 cm by 13 cm white rayon. Face, Nose, Arms, Legs—60 cm by 14 cm cotton jersey. Eyes—dacron georgette. Mouth—strands of embroidery thread. Hair—mohair yarn, 34 cm of 1.8 cm floral braid. Clothes—20 cm by 12.5 cm pale yellow flet, 20 cm of 1.8 cm floral braid. Flute—10 cm of No. 16 wire, Tin foil. Also—No. 18 wire, packing, cotton wadding, polyester batting.

FINISHED SIZE: Refer to diagram.

INSTRUCTIONS:

The basic method is the same as for Hiji, so refer to pages 50-64.

Boys: Make hands and legs with cotton fabric. For the way to stuff hands and legs and the way to set up bodies, refer to page 110. Sew on hair as shown on page 72.

Pose them, bending their arms and legs.

Girl: Make in same manner as for boys. Feature face, secure flute inside her arms.

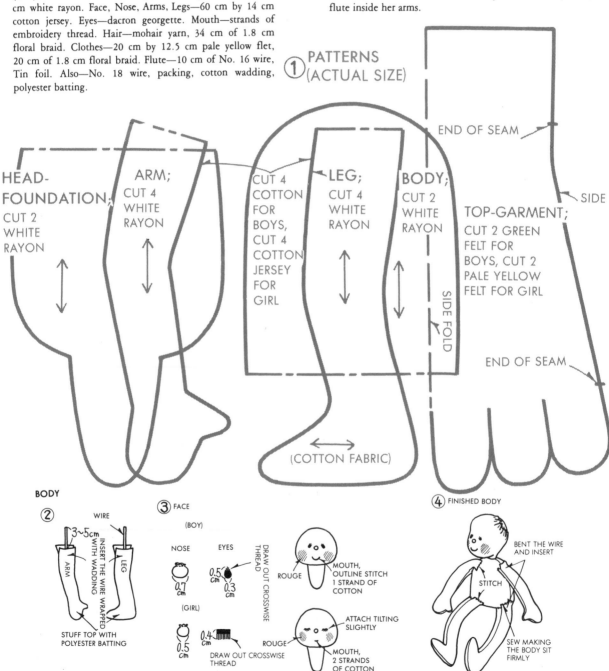

① PATTERNS (ACTUAL SIZE)

HEAD-FOUNDATION; CUT 2 WHITE RAYON

ARM; CUT 4 WHITE RAYON

CUT 4 COTTON FOR BOYS, CUT 4 COTTON JERSEY FOR GIRL

LEG; CUT 4 WHITE RAYON

BODY; CUT 2 WHITE RAYON

END OF SEAM

SIDE

SIDE FOLD

TOP-GARMENT; CUT 2 GREEN FELT FOR BOYS, CUT 2 PALE YELLOW FELT FOR GIRL

END OF SEAM

(COTTON FABRIC)

BODY

② WIRE
3~5 cm
INSERT THE WIRE WRAPPED WITH WADDING
ARM
LEG
STUFF TOP WITH POLYESTER BATTING

③ FACE
(BOY)
NOSE
0.7 cm
EYES
0.5 cm
0.3 cm
DRAW OUT CROSSWISE THREAD
ROUGE
MOUTH, OUTLINE STITCH 1 STRAND OF COTTON

(GIRL)
0.5 cm
0.4 cm
DRAW OUT CROSSWISE THREAD
ROUGE
ATTACH TILTING SLIGHTLY
MOUTH, 2 STRANDS OF COTTON

④ FINISHED BODY
BENT THE WIRE AND INSERT
STITCH
SEW MAKING THE BODY SIT FIRMLY

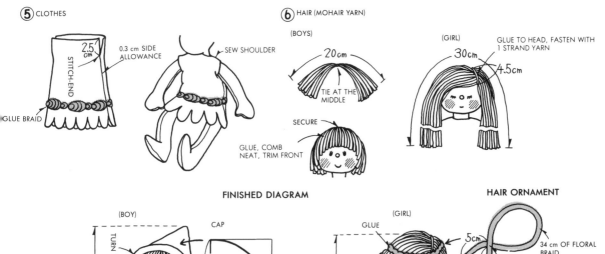

⑤ CLOTHES

2.5 cm
STITCH-END
0.3 cm SIDE ALLOWANCE
GLUE BRAID
SEW SHOULDER

⑥ HAIR (MOHAIR YARN)

(BOYS)
20cm
TIE AT THE MIDDLE
SECURE
GLUE, COMB NEAT, TRIM FRONT

(GIRL)
GLUE TO HEAD, FASTEN WITH 1 STRAND YARN
30cm
4.5cm

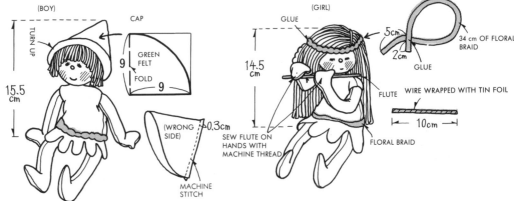

FINISHED DIAGRAM

(BOY)
TURN UP
15.5 Cm
CAP
GREEN FELT
FOLD
9
9
(WRONG SIDE) 0.3cm
SEW FLUTE ON HANDS WITH MACHINE THREAD
MACHINE STITCH

(GIRL)
14.5 cm
GLUE
FLUTE
FLORAL BRAID

HAIR ORNAMENT
5cm
2cm
34 cm OF FLORAL BRAID
GLUE
WIRE WRAPPED WITH TIN FOIL
10cm

THE LAND OF UNBORN BABIES

Shown on pages 26-27.

Make them from the same pattern, and use variety in posing them. Finish the packing neatly, for bodies are used as they are. Emphasize their baby-like poses.

YOU'LL NEED (for each):
Head-Foundation, Body, Arms, Legs—37.5 cm by 17 cm white rayon. Face, Nose, Body, Arms, Legs—28.5 cm by 17 cm cotton jersey. Eyes—dacron georgette. Hair—lightweight yarn. Swaddle—16 cm by 10 cm georgette. Also—No. 18 wire, packing, cotton wadding, polyester batting.
FINISHED SIZE: Refer to diagram.

INSTRUCTIONS:
The basic method is the same as for Hiji, so refer to pages 50-64.
Sew body in the same way as arms and legs, stuff with packing.
Stuff arms and legs, referring to page 110; sew on head, arms and legs for the different position.
Sew on hair as shown on page 72. Pose dolls, bending arms and legs as you see in the picture.

① PATTERNS (ACTUAL SIZE):

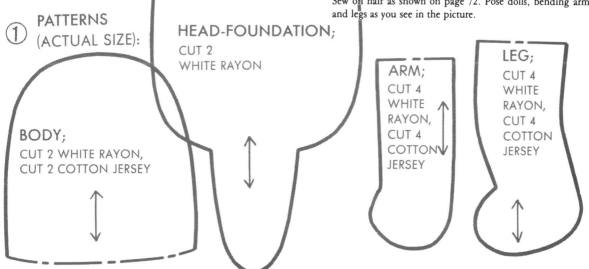

HEAD-FOUNDATION;
CUT 2
WHITE RAYON

BODY;
CUT 2 WHITE RAYON,
CUT 2 COTTON JERSEY

ARM;
CUT 4 WHITE RAYON,
CUT 4 COTTON JERSEY

LEG;
CUT 4 WHITE RAYON,
CUT 4 COTTON JERSEY

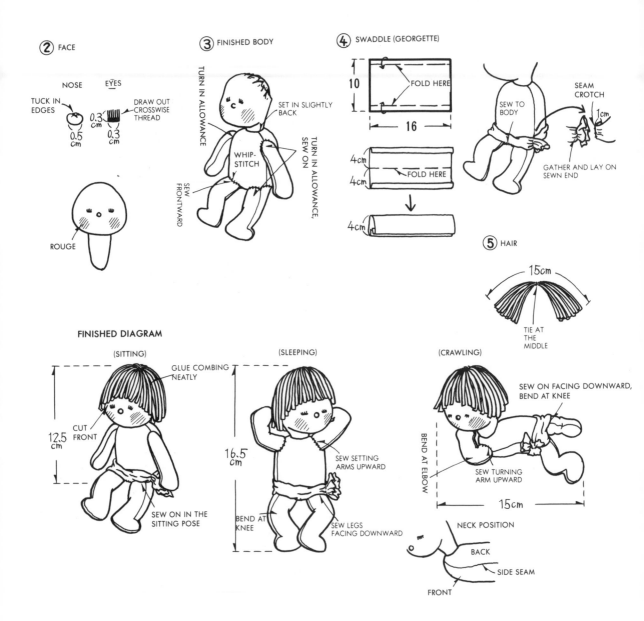

② FACE

NOSE

TUCK IN EDGES

0.5 cm

EYES

0.3 cm   0.3 cm

DRAW OUT CROSSWISE THREAD

ROUGE

③ FINISHED BODY

TURN IN ALLOWANCE

SET IN SLIGHTLY BACK

TURN IN ALLOWANCE, SEW ON

WHIP-STITCH

SEW FRONTWARD

④ SWADDLE (GEORGETTE)

10

16

FOLD HERE

4cm
4cm

FOLD HERE

4cm

SEW TO BODY

SEAM CROTCH

1cm

GATHER AND LAY ON SEWN END

⑤ HAIR

15cm

TIE AT THE MIDDLE

FINISHED DIAGRAM

(SITTING)

GLUE COMBING NEATLY

12.5 cm

CUT FRONT

SEW ON IN THE SITTING POSE

(SLEEPING)

16.5 cm

SEW SETTING ARMS UPWARD

BEND AT KNEE

SEW LEGS FACING DOWNWARD

(CRAWLING)

SEW ON FACING DOWNWARD, BEND AT KNEE

BEND AT ELBOW

SEW TURNING ARM UPWARD

15cm

NECK POSITION

BACK

SIDE SEAM

FRONT

ONDEENA

Shown on page 28.

The choice of materials for hair and dress is the key to making her look nymphlike. Try to get this kind of yarn. Study the balance of arms and legs in the way she is posed.

YOU'LL NEED:
Head-Foundation, Body, Arms, Legs—80 cm by 37 cm white rayon. Face, Nose, Body, Arms, Legs—80 cm by 40 cm cotton jersey. Body—24 cm by 22 cm white georgette. Eyes—dacron georgette. Mouth—strands of embroidery thread. Hair—white lamé yarn, artificial flower. Dress—50 cm by 45 cm white georgette, 17 cm of 1.8 cm braid. Bouquet—artificial flower. Also—100 cm of 0.4 cm ribbon, No. 18 wire, packing, cotton wadding, polyester batting, 13 cm of white elastic.
FINISHED SIZE: Refer to diagram.

INSTRUCTIONS;
The basic method is the same as for Hiji, so refer to pages 50-64.
Make body with white rayon, overlapping cotton jersey and then georgette.
Make arms and legs, referring to page 107. Cut out soles, stitch in place.
Put on dress, belt the waist. Bundle a little of the hair on right side, glue on hair ornament.
Bend arms and legs as shown; sew bouquet on hands, secure legs at knee to steady doll.

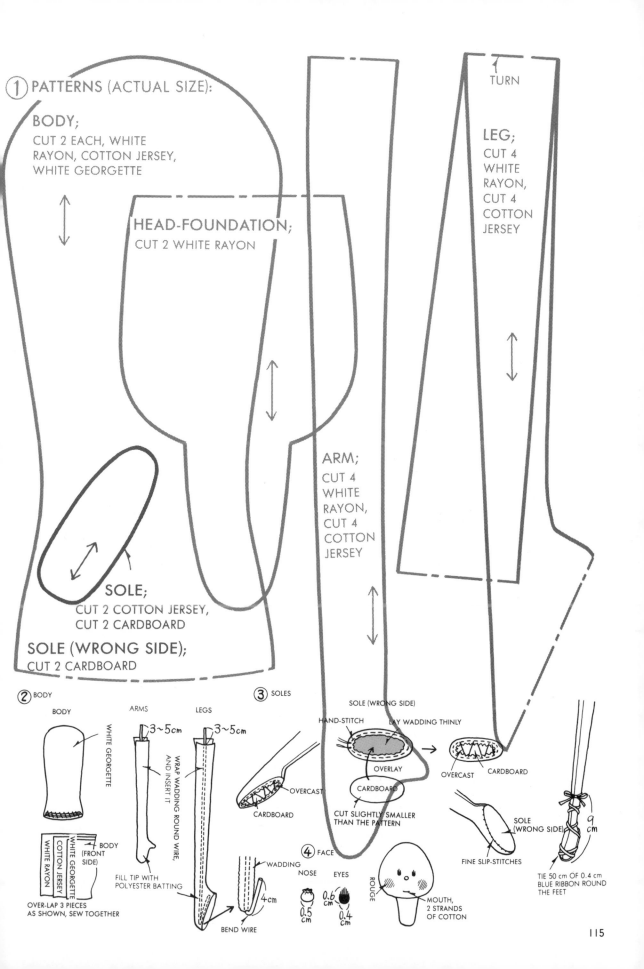

① PATTERNS (ACTUAL SIZE):

BODY;
CUT 2 EACH, WHITE
RAYON, COTTON JERSEY,
WHITE GEORGETTE

HEAD-FOUNDATION;
CUT 2 WHITE RAYON

LEG;
CUT 4
WHITE
RAYON,
CUT 4
COTTON
JERSEY

TURN

ARM;
CUT 4
WHITE
RAYON,
CUT 4
COTTON
JERSEY

SOLE;
CUT 2 COTTON JERSEY,
CUT 2 CARDBOARD

SOLE (WRONG SIDE);
CUT 2 CARDBOARD

② BODY

BODY

WHITE GEORGETTE

ARMS   LEGS

3~5cm   3~5cm

WRAP WADDING ROUND WIRE,
AND INSERT IT

BODY
(FRONT
SIDE)

WHITE GEORGETTE
COTTON JERSEY
WHITE RAYON

OVER-LAP 3 PIECES
AS SHOWN, SEW TOGETHER

FILL TIP WITH
POLYESTER BATTING

WADDING

4cm

BEND WIRE

③ SOLES

SOLE (WRONG SIDE)

HAND-STITCH   LAY WADDING THINLY

OVERLAY

CARDBOARD

OVERCAST

CARDBOARD

CUT SLIGHTLY SMALLER
THAN THE PATTERN

OVERCAST   CARDBOARD

SOLE
(WRONG SIDE)

FINE SLIP-STITCHES

9
cm

TIE 50 cm OF 0.4 cm
BLUE RIBBON ROUND
THE FEET

④ FACE

NOSE   EYES

0.6
cm
0.5
cm

0.4
cm

ROUGE

MOUTH,
2 STRANDS
OF COTTON

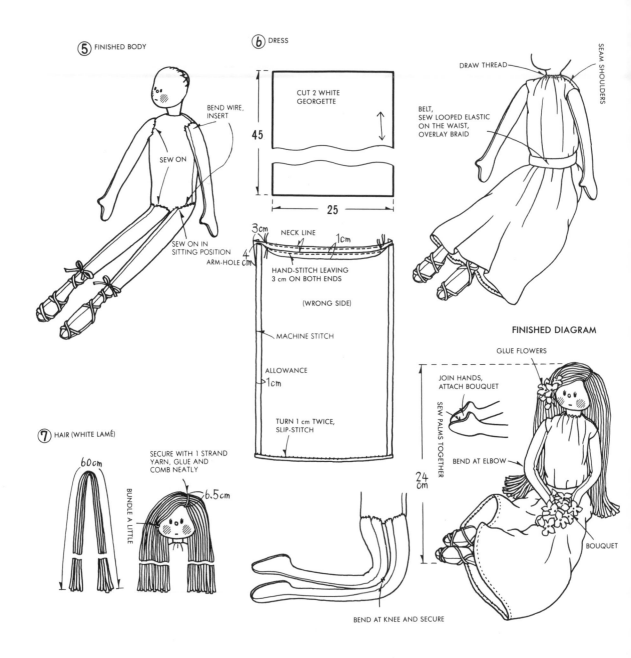

⑤ FINISHED BODY

BEND WIRE, INSERT

SEW ON

SEW ON IN SITTING POSITION

⑥ DRESS

CUT 2 WHITE GEORGETTE

45

25

3cm NECK LINE 1cm
ARM-HOLE 4cm
HAND-STITCH LEAVING 3 cm ON BOTH ENDS

(WRONG SIDE)

MACHINE STITCH

ALLOWANCE 1cm

TURN 1 cm TWICE, SLIP-STITCH

DRAW THREAD

SEAM SHOULDERS

BELT, SEW LOOPED ELASTIC ON THE WAIST, OVERLAY BRAID

FINISHED DIAGRAM

⑦ HAIR (WHITE LAMÉ)

60cm

BUNDLE A LITTLE

SECURE WITH 1 STRAND YARN, GLUE AND COMB NEATLY

6.5cm

GLUE FLOWERS

JOIN HANDS, ATTACH BOUQUET

SEW PALMS TOGETHER

BEND AT ELBOW

24 cm

BEND AT KNEE AND SECURE

BOUQUET

PUCK

Shown on page 29.

Stuff packing neatly to give a smooth finish to the body. Emphasize the mischievous spirit of this love-messenger in his features and pose.

YOU'LL NEED:
Head-Foundation, Body, Arms, Legs—60 cm by 32 cm white rayon. Face, Nose—12 cm by 15 cm beige cotton jersey. Body, Arms, Legs—70 cm by 28 cm white cotton jersey. Eyes—dacron georgette, gold lamé yarn. Mouth—strands of embroidery thread. Hair-bouclé. Also—artificial leaves, green taped wire, No. 18 wire, packing, cotton wadding, polyester batting.
FINISHED SIZE: Refer to diagram.

INSTRUCTIONS:
Make body, arms, and legs of white jeresey. For the way to make arms and legs, refer to page 107. Attach soles after the green wire is tied round legs. Hair is made of bouclé softly crocheted with single crochet using No. G hook needle, and used on its reverse side. Put polyester batting in the crocheted hair and pull over the head.
Attach leaves to the body, and pose doll by bending arms and legs.

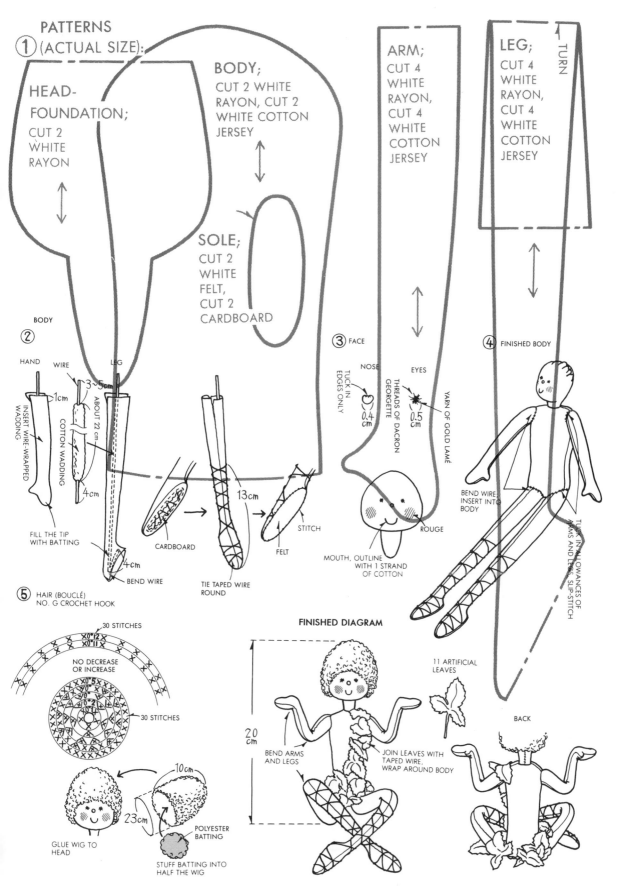

PATTERNS
① (ACTUAL SIZE):

HEAD-
FOUNDATION;
CUT 2
WHITE
RAYON

BODY;
CUT 2 WHITE
RAYON, CUT 2
WHITE COTTON
JERSEY

SOLE;
CUT 2
WHITE
FELT,
CUT 2
CARDBOARD

ARM;
CUT 4
WHITE
RAYON,
CUT 4
WHITE
COTTON
JERSEY

LEG;
CUT 4
WHITE
RAYON,
CUT 4
WHITE
COTTON
JERSEY

TURN

BODY
②

HAND
WIRE
LEG
3~5cm
ABOUT 22 cm
1cm
COTTON
WADDING
INSERT WIRE-WRAPPED
WADDING
4cm
FILL THE TIP
WITH BATTING
4cm
BEND WIRE

CARDBOARD

13cm
TIE TAPED WIRE
ROUND
STITCH
FELT

③ FACE
NOSE
TUCK IN
EDGES ONLY
0.4
cm
THREADS OF DACRON
GEORGETTE
EYES
0.5
cm
YARN OF GOLD LAMÉ
ROUGE
MOUTH, OUTLINE
WITH 1 STRAND
OF COTTON

④ FINISHED BODY
BEND WIRE;
INSERT INTO
BODY
TUCK IN ALLOWANCES OF
ARMS AND LEGS, SLIP-STITCH

⑤ HAIR (BOUCLÉ)
NO. G CROCHET HOOK

30 STITCHES
X0"12 X
X0"11 X
NO DECREASE
OR INCREASE
X0"5 X
X0"3
X0"2
30 STITCHES

GLUE WIG TO
HEAD

10cm
23cm
POLYESTER
BATTING
STUFF BATTING INTO
HALF THE WIG

FINISHED DIAGRAM

20
cm

BEND ARMS
AND LEGS

11 ARTIFICIAL
LEAVES

JOIN LEAVES WITH
TAPED WIRE,
WRAP AROUND BODY

BACK

117

PIPPI LONGSTOCKING

Shown on page 30.

Though arms and legs look short in the picture, she really has a smart figure. Insert wire into hair braided on the sides and bend up to give her a rompish look.

YOU'LL NEED:

Head-Foundation, Body, Arms, Legs—90 cm by 30 cm white rayon. Face, Nose, Arms—40 cm by 25 cm beige cotton jersey. Legs—20 cm by 30 cm each, black cotton Jersey, dark brown cotton jersey. Eyes—dacron georgette. Mouth—stands of embroidery thread. Hair—sport-weight yarn. Dress, Bloomer—54.5 cm by 24 cm dotted print cotton, strands of embroidery cotton. Scarf—30 cm by 12 cm cotton print. Also—No. 18 wire, packing, cotton wadding, polyester batting.

FINISHED SIZE: Refer to diagram.

INSTRUCTIONS:

Referring to pages 50-64 for basic method, make legs of black and dark brown respectively.

Tuck garment at center front, sew on decorated pocket, stitch side seams.

Sew on hair in same manner as for Hiji, insert wire into hair braided on sides and bend as shown.

Cut out scarf piece, wrap round neck.

Make shoes sewing on feet, finish by bending their tops upward. Bend legs if you like, securing at the knee back side in same manner as toe.

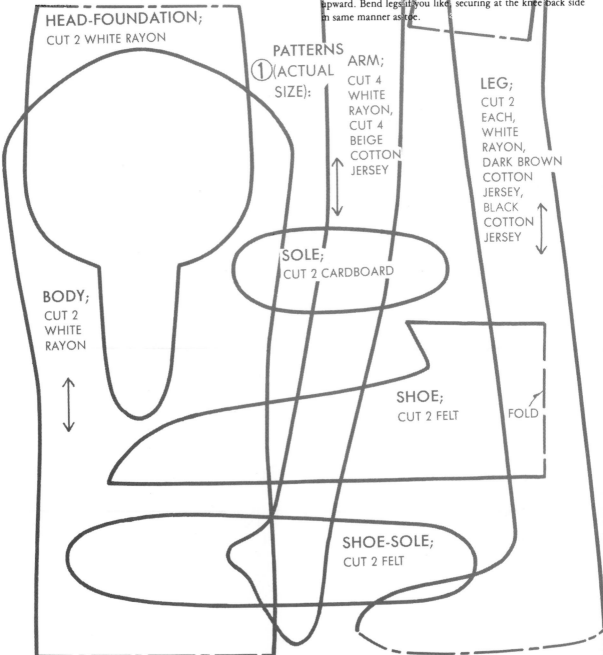

HEAD-FOUNDATION;
CUT 2 WHITE RAYON

PATTERNS
①(ACTUAL SIZE):

ARM;
CUT 4 WHITE RAYON, CUT 4 BEIGE COTTON JERSEY

LEG;
CUT 2 EACH, WHITE RAYON, DARK BROWN COTTON JERSEY, BLACK COTTON JERSEY

BODY;
CUT 2 WHITE RAYON

SOLE;
CUT 2 CARDBOARD

SHOE;
CUT 2 FELT

FOLD

SHOE-SOLE;
CUT 2 FELT

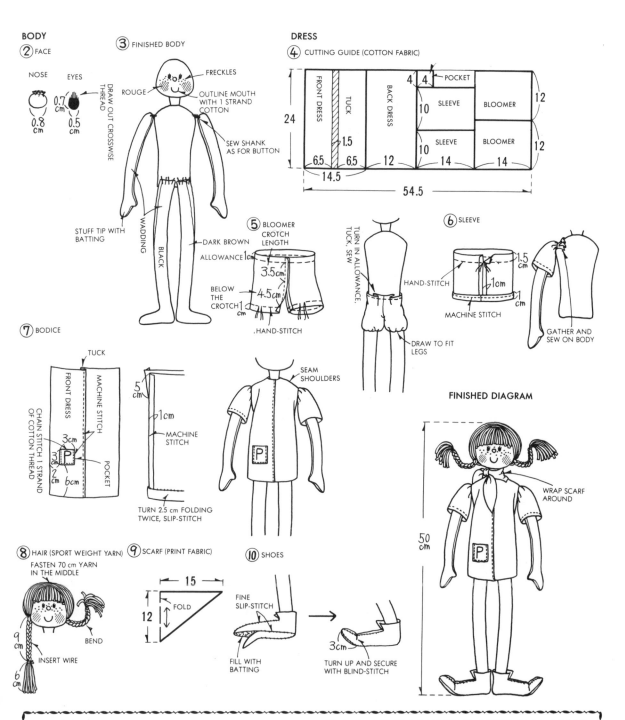

BODY

② FACE

NOSE EYES

0.7 cm 0.5 cm
0.8 cm

③ FINISHED BODY

FRECKLES
ROUGE
OUTLINE MOUTH WITH 1 STRAND COTTON
DRAW OUT CROSSWISE THREAD
SEW SHANK AS FOR BUTTON
STUFF TIP WITH BATTING
WADDING
BLACK
DARK BROWN

DRESS

④ CUTTING GUIDE (COTTON FABRIC)

FRONT DRESS | TUCK | BACK DRESS | 4 4 POCKET
10 SLEEVE | BLOOMER | 12
10 SLEEVE | BLOOMER | 12
24
1.5
6.5 6.5 12 14 14
14.5
54.5

⑤ BLOOMER
CROTCH LENGTH
ALLOWANCE 1cm
3.5cm
4.5cm
BELOW THE CROTCH 1cm
HAND-STITCH

TURN IN ALLOWANCE, TUCK, SEW.
DRAW TO FIT LEGS

⑥ SLEEVE
HAND-STITCH
1cm
1.5 cm
1
MACHINE STITCH
GATHER AND SEW ON BODY

⑦ BODICE
TUCK
FRONT DRESS
MACHINE STITCH
CHAIN STITCH 1 STRAND OF COTTON THREAD
3cm
P
2cm 6cm
POCKET
5 cm
1cm
MACHINE STITCH
TURN 2.5 cm FOLDING TWICE, SLIP-STITCH

SEAM SHOULDERS
P

FINISHED DIAGRAM

WRAP SCARF AROUND
50 cm
P

⑧ HAIR (SPORT WEIGHT YARN)
FASTEN 70 cm YARN IN THE MIDDLE
9 cm
INSERT WIRE
6 cm
BEND

⑨ SCARF (PRINT FABRIC)
15
12
FOLD

⑩ SHOES
FINE SLIP-STITCH
FILL WITH BATTING
3cm
TURN UP AND SECURE WITH BLIND-STITCH

LOTTA

Shown on page 31.

To make a stubbon' mischievous child, do a rough hair-cut. Put on stockings as if right side slipped down loosely. The sweater beside her is only an accessory.

YOU'LL NEED:
Head-Foundation, Body, Arms, Legs—90 cm by 14.5 cm white rayon. Face, Nose, Body, Arms, Legs—82 cm by 16 cm cotton jersey. Eyes—dacron georgette. Mouth—strands of embroidery thread. Hair—mohair yarn. Shirt, Pants—13.5 cm by 36 cm cotton print. Stockings—lightweight yarn pale yellow, olive green. Sweater—Lightweight yarn gray. Pig—15 cm by 5 cm felt, dacron georgette. Also—No. 18

wire, packing, cotton wadding, polyester batting.
FINISHED SIZE: Refer to diagram.
INSTRUCTIONS;
Referring to pages 50-64 for basic method, make arms and legs in same manner as for Puck on page 117.
Make hair as shown on page 72, finish with laddercut. Additional yarn for hair is attached on sides and back.
Crochet sweater and stockings with size 1 hook.

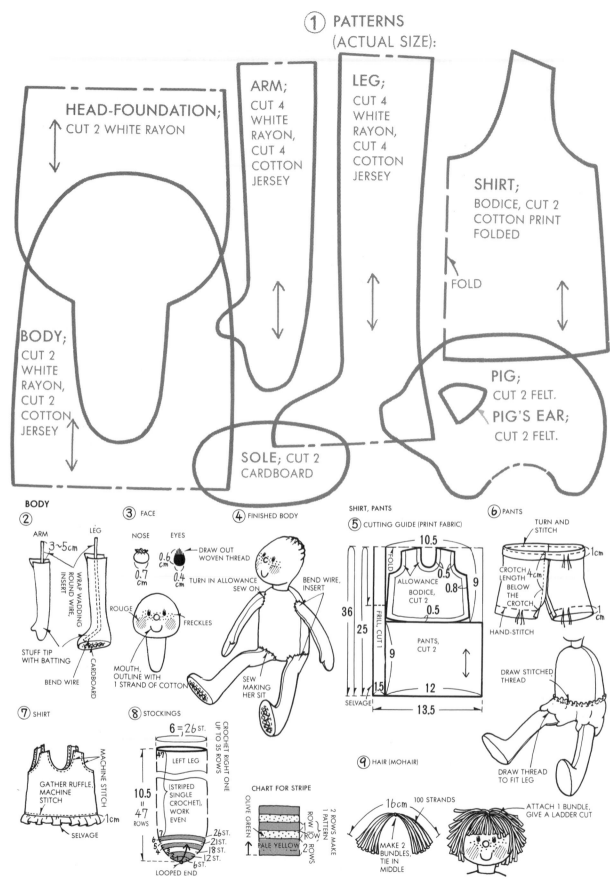

① PATTERNS (ACTUAL SIZE):

HEAD-FOUNDATION;
CUT 2 WHITE RAYON

ARM;
CUT 4 WHITE RAYON,
CUT 4 COTTON JERSEY

LEG;
CUT 4 WHITE RAYON,
CUT 4 COTTON JERSEY

SHIRT;
BODICE, CUT 2 COTTON PRINT FOLDED

FOLD

BODY;
CUT 2 WHITE RAYON,
CUT 2 COTTON JERSEY

SOLE; CUT 2 CARDBOARD

PIG;
CUT 2 FELT.

PIG'S EAR;
CUT 2 FELT.

BODY

②

ARM
LEG
3~5cm

WRAP WADDING ROUND WIRE, INSERT

STUFF TIP WITH BATTING

BEND WIRE

CARDBOARD

③ FACE

NOSE
0.7 cm

EYES
0.6 cm
0.4 cm
DRAW OUT WOVEN THREAD
TURN IN ALLOWANCE SEW ON

ROUGE
FRECKLES

MOUTH, OUTLINE WITH 1 STRAND OF COTTON

④ FINISHED BODY

BEND WIRE, INSERT

SEW MAKING HER SIT

SHIRT, PANTS

⑤ CUTTING GUIDE (PRINT FABRIC)

10.5

FOLD

ALLOWANCE
BODICE, CUT 2
0.5
0.8
0.5
9

36
25
FRILL, CUT 1

PANTS, CUT 2
9

1.5
12
13.5

SELVAGE

⑥ PANTS

TURN AND STITCH
1cm

CROTCH LENGTH 4cm BELOW THE CROTCH
1cm

HAND-STITCH

DRAW STITCHED THREAD

DRAW THREAD TO FIT LEG

⑦ SHIRT

MACHINE STITCH

GATHER RUFFLE, MACHINE STITCH

SELVAGE
1cm

⑧ STOCKINGS

6 = 26 ST.

47

LEFT LEG

CROCHET RIGHT ONE UP TO 35 ROWS

(STRIPED SINGLE CROCHET), WORK EVEN

10.5 = 47 ROWS

47
6
5
4
3

26 ST.
21 ST.
18 ST.
12 ST.
6 ST.

LOOPED END

CHART FOR STRIPE

OLIVE GREEN
PALE YELLOW

ROW ROW
2 ROWS MAKE 1 PATTERN

⑨ HAIR (MOHAIR)

16cm
100 STRANDS

MAKE 2 BUNDLES, TIE IN MIDDLE

ATTACH 1 BUNDLE, GIVE A LADDER CUT

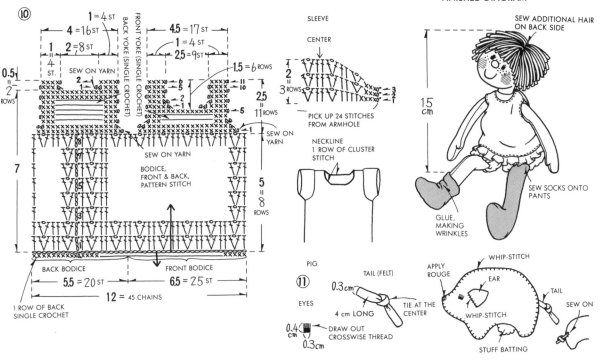

⑩

1 = 4 ST
4 = 16 ST
1
4 ST.
2 = 8 ST
BACK YOKE (SINGLE CROCHET)
FRONT YOKE (SINGLE CROCHET)
4.5 = 17 ST
1 = 4 ST
2.5 = 9 ST
1.5 = 6 ROWS
0.5
2 ROWS
SEW ON YARN
2.5
11 ROWS
SEW ON YARN
7
SEW ON YARN
BODICE, FRONT & BACK, PATTERN STITCH
5
8 ROWS
BACK BODICE
FRONT BODICE
5.5 = 20 ST
6.5 = 25 ST
12 = 45 CHAINS
1 ROW OF BACK SINGLE CROCHET

SLEEVE
CENTER
2
3 ROWS
1
PICK UP 24 STITCHES FROM ARMHOLE
NECKLINE
1 ROW OF CLUSTER STITCH

SEW ADDITIONAL HAIR ON BACK SIDE
15 cm
SEW SOCKS ONTO PANTS
GLUE, MAKING WRINKLES

PIG
⑪
EYES
TAIL (FELT)
0.3 cm
4 cm LONG
TIE AT THE CENTER
0.4 cm
DRAW OUT CROSSWISE THREAD
0.3 cm

APPLY ROUGE
WHIP-STITCH
EAR
TAIL
SEW ON
WHIP-STITCH
STUFF BATTING

GYPSY

Shown on page 32.

Use care when drawing the thread of wrinkles on her face. The hair is made of yarn unraveled from knit work. Emphasize her figure, making it thick through breast, waist, and hips.

YOU'LL NEED:
Head-Foundation, Body, Arms, Legs—82 cm by 24 cm white rayon. Face, Nose, Arms—35 cm by 17 cm beige cotton jersey. Legs—28 cm by 12 cm black cotton jersey. Eyes—dacron georgette. Mouth—strands of embroidery thread. Hair—white knitting cotton. Bloomer, Petticoat—70 cm by 15 cm white broadcloth, 80 cm of 2 cm white lace. Dress, Scarf—65 cm by 48 cm tricot print. 30 cm of 1.5 cm black lace, heavyweight yarn. Earrings—silver and black braid. Shoes—24 cm of 2.5 cm braid. Stole—No. 30 black lace, Silver lamé yarn. Also—No. 12 silk necklace, No. 18 wire, packing, cotton wadding, polyester batting.

FINISHED SIZE: Refer to diagram.
INSTRUCTIONS:
Referring to pages 50-64 for basic method, make arms and legs in same manner as for Prince on page 107.
Lay wadding over face for more prominent cheeks and jaw; overlay skin fabric and stitch wrinkles with silk thread.
Lay wadding over the breast, waist, and hips to make them thick, sew on underwear and then dress.
Make hair of yarn unraveled from some knit work and attach on the head as shown.
Crochet scarf with a size 8 hook.

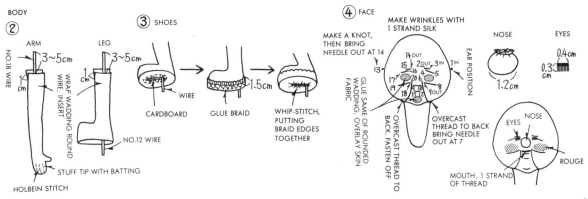

BODY
②
ARM
NO.18 WIRE
3~5 cm
1 cm
WRAP WADDING ROUND WIRE, INSERT
STUFF TIP WITH BATTING
HOLBEIN STITCH

LEG
3~5 cm
1 cm
NO.12 WIRE

③ SHOES
WIRE
CARDBOARD
GLUE BRAID
1.5 cm
WHIP-STITCH, PUTTING BRAID EDGES TOGETHER

④ FACE
MAKE WRINKLES WITH 1 STRAND SILK
MAKE A KNOT, THEN BRING NEEDLE OUT AT 14
GLUE SAME OR ROUNDED WADDING, OVERLAY SKIN FABRIC
EAR POSITION
OVERCAST THREAD TO BACK, FASTEN OFF
OVERCAST THREAD TO BACK BRING NEEDLE OUT AT 7
MOUTH, 1 STRAND OF THREAD

NOSE
1.2 cm

EYES
0.4 cm
0.3 cm

EYES
NOSE
ROUGE

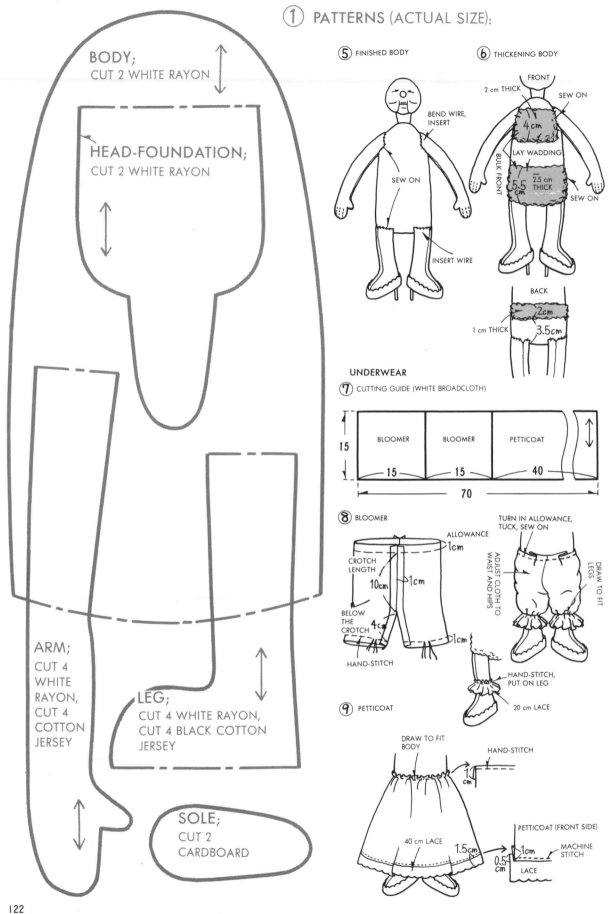

① PATTERNS (ACTUAL SIZE):

BODY;
CUT 2 WHITE RAYON

HEAD-FOUNDATION;
CUT 2 WHITE RAYON

ARM;
CUT 4
WHITE
RAYON,
CUT 4
COTTON
JERSEY

LEG;
CUT 4 WHITE RAYON,
CUT 4 BLACK COTTON
JERSEY

SOLE;
CUT 2
CARDBOARD

⑤ FINISHED BODY

BEND WIRE,
INSERT

SEW ON

INSERT WIRE

⑥ THICKENING BODY

FRONT
2 cm THICK
SEW ON
4 cm
LAY WADDING
BULK FRONT
5.5   2.5 cm THICK
SEW ON

BACK
2 cm
1 cm THICK
3.5 cm

UNDERWEAR

⑦ CUTTING GUIDE (WHITE BROADCLOTH)

15

BLOOMER	BLOOMER	PETTICOAT
15	15	40

70

⑧ BLOOMER

ALLOWANCE
1cm
CROTCH
LENGTH
10cm   1cm
BELOW
THE
CROTCH
4cm
HAND-STITCH
1cm

TURN IN ALLOWANCE,
TUCK, SEW ON
ADJUST CLOTH TO WAIST AND HIPS
DRAW TO FIT LEGS

HAND-STITCH,
PUT ON LEG
20 cm LACE

⑨ PETTICOAT

DRAW TO FIT BODY
HAND-STITCH
1 cm

40 cm LACE   1.5cm

PETTICOAT (FRONT SIDE)
1cm
MACHINE STITCH
0.5 cm
LACE

DRESS

⑩ CUTTING GUIDE (TRICOT)

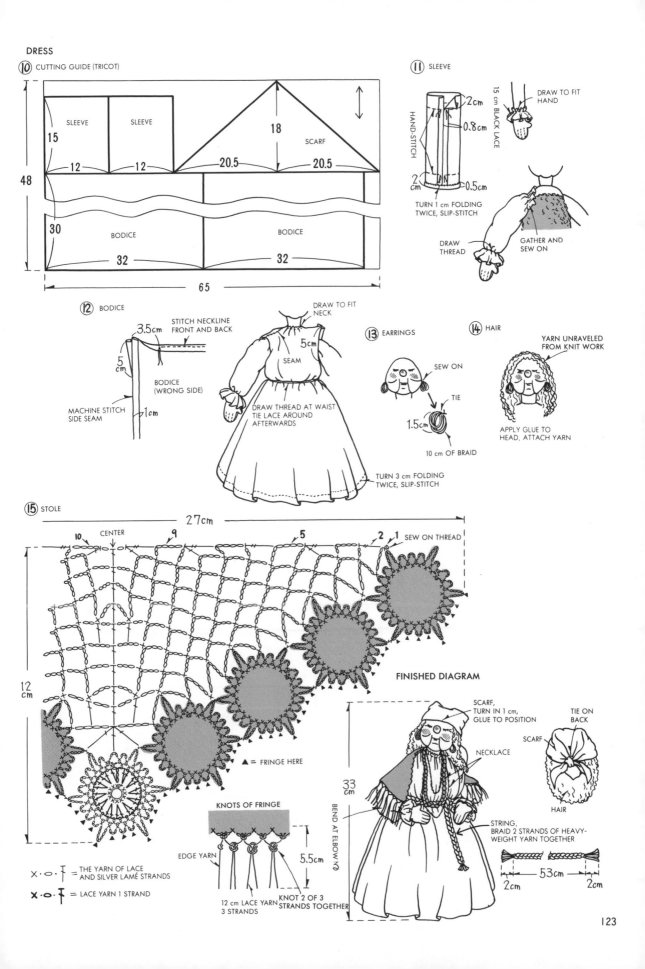

SLEEVE | SLEEVE
15
12 | 12
48
SCARF
18
20.5 | 20.5

30
BODICE | BODICE
32 | 32
65

⑪ SLEEVE

2cm
0.8cm
HAND-STITCH
15 cm BLACK LACE
DRAW TO FIT HAND
2cm | 0.5cm
TURN 1 cm FOLDING TWICE, SLIP-STITCH
DRAW THREAD
GATHER AND SEW ON

⑫ BODICE

3.5cm
STITCH NECKLINE FRONT AND BACK
5cm
5cm
DRAW TO FIT NECK
SEAM
BODICE (WRONG SIDE)
MACHINE STITCH SIDE SEAM
1cm
DRAW THREAD AT WAIST TIE LACE AROUND AFTERWARDS
TURN 3 cm FOLDING TWICE, SLIP-STITCH

⑬ EARRINGS

SEW ON
TIE
1.5cm
10 cm OF BRAID

⑭ HAIR

YARN UNRAVELED FROM KNIT WORK
APPLY GLUE TO HEAD, ATTACH YARN

⑮ STOLE

27cm
10   CENTER   9   5   2 1   SEW ON THREAD
12cm
FINISHED DIAGRAM
▲ = FRINGE HERE

KNOTS OF FRINGE

EDGE YARN
5.5cm
12 cm LACE YARN 3 STRANDS
KNOT 2 OF 3 STRANDS TOGETHER

X · O · ⊤ = THE YARN OF LACE AND SILVER LAMÉ STRANDS

X · O · ⊤ = LACE YARN 1 STRAND

SCARF, TURN IN 1 cm, GLUE TO POSITION
NECKLACE
TIE ON BACK
SCARF
HAIR
33cm
BEND AT ELBOW
STRING, BRAID 2 STRANDS OF HEAVY-WEIGHT YARN TOGETHER
2cm   53cm   2cm

THE WITCH OF THE NEW MOON

Shown on page 33.

Her broomstick is made of a tree branch. Try to hang the doll in the air with the string tied on her head, then you can enjoy this flying figure.

YOU'LL NEED:

Head-Foundation, Body, Arms, Legs—77 cm by 25 cm white rayon. Face, Nose, Arms—32 cm by 22 cm beige cotton jersey. Legs—28 cm by 25 cm black cotton jersey. Eyes—dacron georgette. Mouth—strands of embroidery thread. Hair—frizzle yarn. Glasses—black wire. Dress—42 cm by 30 cm black cotton jersey. Cap—19 cm by 16 cm black felt. Broom—45 cm of tree branch, 17 cm square linen. Also—packing, cotton wadding, polyester batting, silk thread, No. 18 wire.

FINISHED SIZE: Refer to diagram.

INSTRUCTIONS:

Referring to pages 50-64 for basic method, make arms and legs in same manner as for Lost Angels shown on page 110. Make wrinkles on her face with silk thread.

Having sewn sleeves on arms, set arms in position. Sew on hair, referring to page 72.

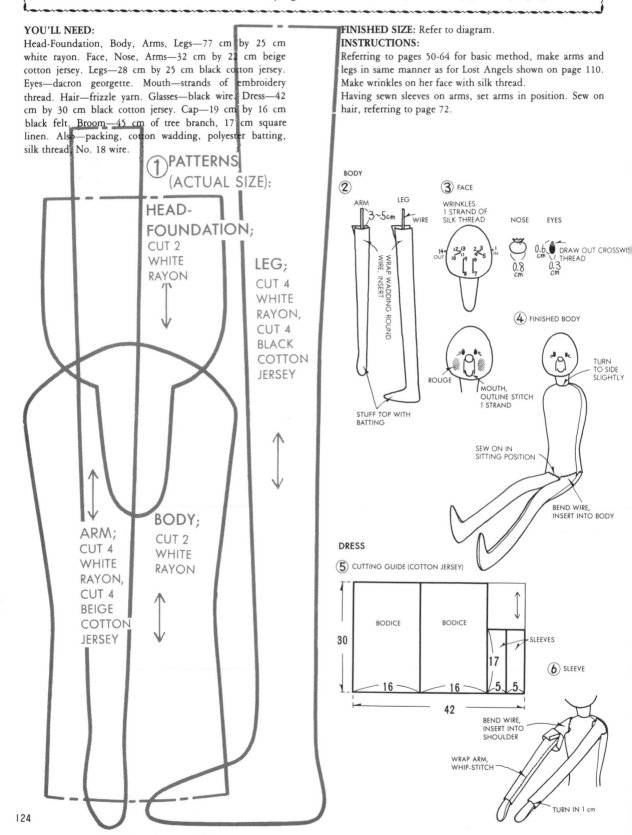

① PATTERNS (ACTUAL SIZE):

HEAD-FOUNDATION; CUT 2 WHITE RAYON

LEG; CUT 4 WHITE RAYON, CUT 4 BLACK COTTON JERSEY

ARM; CUT 4 WHITE RAYON, CUT 4 BEIGE COTTON JERSEY

BODY; CUT 2 WHITE RAYON

② BODY

ARM   LEG   3~5cm   WIRE

WRAP WADDING ROUND WIRE, INSERT

STUFF TOP WITH BATTING

③ FACE

WRINKLES 1 STRAND OF SILK THREAD   NOSE   EYES

14 OUT   12 13   2 3   1 IN   0.6 cm   DRAW OUT CROSSWISE THREAD

0.8 cm   0.3 cm

ROUGE

MOUTH, OUTLINE STITCH 1 STRAND

④ FINISHED BODY

TURN TO SIDE SLIGHTLY

SEW ON IN SITTING POSITION

BEND WIRE, INSERT INTO BODY

DRESS

⑤ CUTTING GUIDE (COTTON JERSEY)

BODICE   BODICE   SLEEVES

30   17

16   16   5   5

42

⑥ SLEEVE

BEND WIRE, INSERT INTO SHOULDER

WRAP ARM, WHIP-STITCH

TURN IN 1 cm

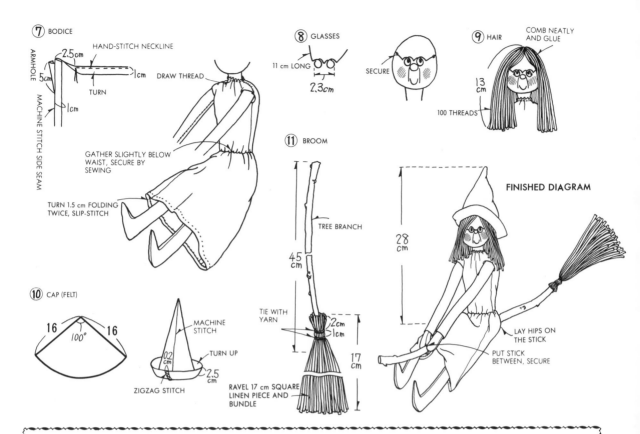

⑦ BODICE

HAND-STITCH NECKLINE

ARMHOLE
2.5cm
5cm
1cm
MACHINE STITCH SIDE SEAM
TURN
1cm
DRAW THREAD

GATHER SLIGHTLY BELOW WAIST, SECURE BY SEWING

TURN 1.5 cm FOLDING TWICE, SLIP-STITCH

⑧ GLASSES
11 cm LONG
2.3cm
SECURE

⑨ HAIR
COMB NEATLY AND GLUE
13 cm
100 THREADS

⑪ BROOM

TREE BRANCH
45 cm
TIE WITH YARN
2cm
1cm
17 cm

FINISHED DIAGRAM
28 cm
LAY HIPS ON THE STICK
PUT STICK BETWEEN, SECURE

⑩ CAP (FELT)
16   16
100°
MACHINE STITCH
0.2 cm
TURN UP
2.5 cm
ZIGZAG STITCH

RAVEL 17 cm SQUARE LINEN PIECE AND BUNDLE

AUNT HETTY

Shown on page 34.

Hairs are unraveled old yarn. Let her stand, making holes on a board 2.5 cm or higher with gimlet. Make wrinkles by drawing thread slightly.

YOU'LL NEED:
Head-Foundation, Body, Arms—47 cm by 27 cm white rayon. Face, Nose, Arms—50 cm by 27 cm cotton jersey. Legs—18 cm by 28 cm striped cotton. Eyes—dacron georgette. Mouth—strands of embroidery thread. Hair—mohair yarn. Glasses—gray wire. Bloomer, Petticoat, Apron, Blouse's collar, Front Placket—59 cm by 23 cm white broadcloth, 51 cm of 2.5 cm white lace, 13 cm of 1.5 cm white lace. Blouse—36 cm by 18 cm cotton seersucker, 25 cm of 3 cm lace. Skirt—30 cm by 25 cm denim. Shoes—26 cm by 3 cm velveteen, 5 cm by 4 cm felt. Also—wire No. 12, No. 18; packing, cotton wadding, polyester batting, silk thread.

FINISHED SIZE: Refer to diagram.
INSTRUCTIONS:
Make according to basic manner on pages 50-64.
Attach skin fabric to face after wadding piece is laid on cheeks and jaw, then stitch wrinkles with silk thread. Make arms and legs with inserted wire. Shoes are made as shown on page 90. For the hair, use the yarn unraveled from knit goods, attaching to the head with glue.

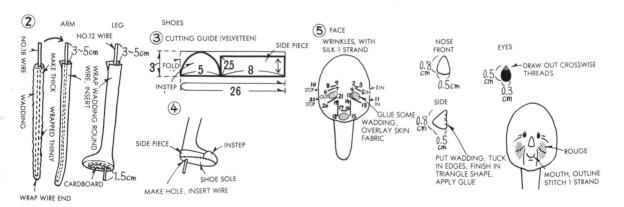

② ARM   LEG   SHOES
NO.12 WIRE
NO.18 WIRE
3~5cm   3~5cm
MAKE THICK
WRAPPED THINLY
WRAP WADDING ROUND, WIRE, INSERT
WADDING
CARDBOARD
1.5cm
WRAP WIRE END

③ CUTTING GUIDE (VELVETEEN)
SIDE PIECE
3   FOLD   5   25   8
INSTEP   26

④
SIDE PIECE   INSTEP
SHOE SOLE
MAKE HOLE, INSERT WIRE

⑤ FACE
WRINKLES, WITH SILK 1 STRAND
GLUE SOME WADDING, OVERLAY SKIN FABRIC

NOSE
FRONT
0.8 cm
0.5cm
SIDE
0.8 cm
0.5 cm
PUT WADDING, TUCK IN EDGES, FINISH IN TRIANGLE SHAPE, APPLY GLUE

EYES
DRAW OUT CROSSWISE THREADS
0.5 cm
0.3 cm
ROUGE
MOUTH, OUTLINE STITCH 1 STRAND

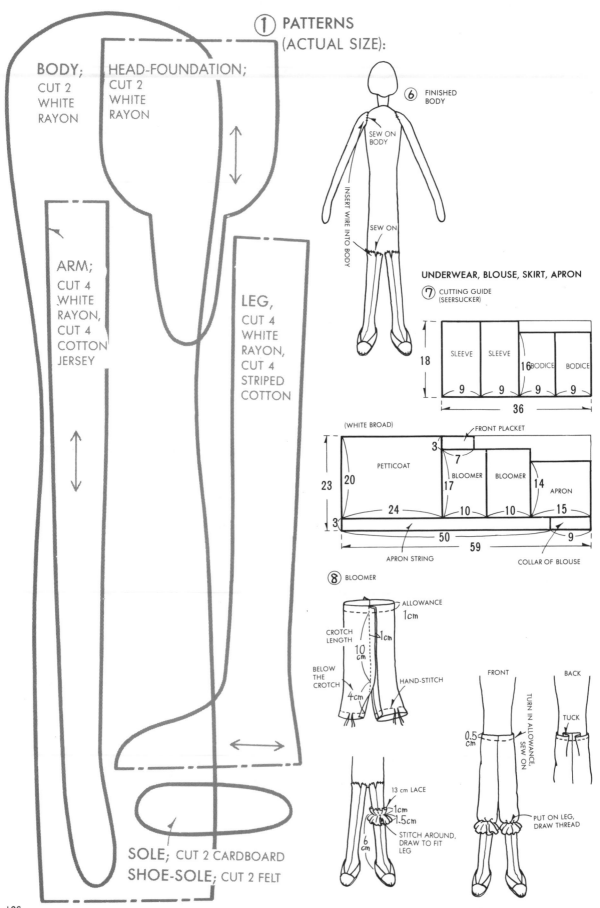

① PATTERNS
(ACTUAL SIZE):

BODY;
CUT 2
WHITE
RAYON

HEAD-FOUNDATION;
CUT 2
WHITE
RAYON

ARM;
CUT 4
WHITE
RAYON,
CUT 4
COTTON
JERSEY

LEG,
CUT 4
WHITE
RAYON,
CUT 4
STRIPED
COTTON

SOLE; CUT 2 CARDBOARD
SHOE-SOLE; CUT 2 FELT

⑥ FINISHED BODY

SEW ON BODY

INSERT WIRE INTO BODY

SEW ON

UNDERWEAR, BLOUSE, SKIRT, APRON

⑦ CUTTING GUIDE (SEERSUCKER)

		16	
SLEEVE	SLEEVE	BODICE	BODICE
9	9	9	9

18

36

(WHITE BROAD)

FRONT PLACKET

PETTICOAT		3 7			
20		BLOOMER 17	BLOOMER	14	APRON
24		10	10	15	

3

23

3

50

59

9

APRON STRING

COLLAR OF BLOUSE

⑧ BLOOMER

ALLOWANCE
1cm

CROTCH
LENGTH

1cm

10 cm

BELOW
THE
CROTCH

4cm

HAND-STITCH

FRONT

BACK

TURN IN ALLOWANCE,
SEW ON

TUCK

0.5 cm

13 cm LACE

1cm
1.5cm

6 cm

STITCH AROUND,
DRAW TO FIT
LEG

PUT ON LEG,
DRAW THREAD

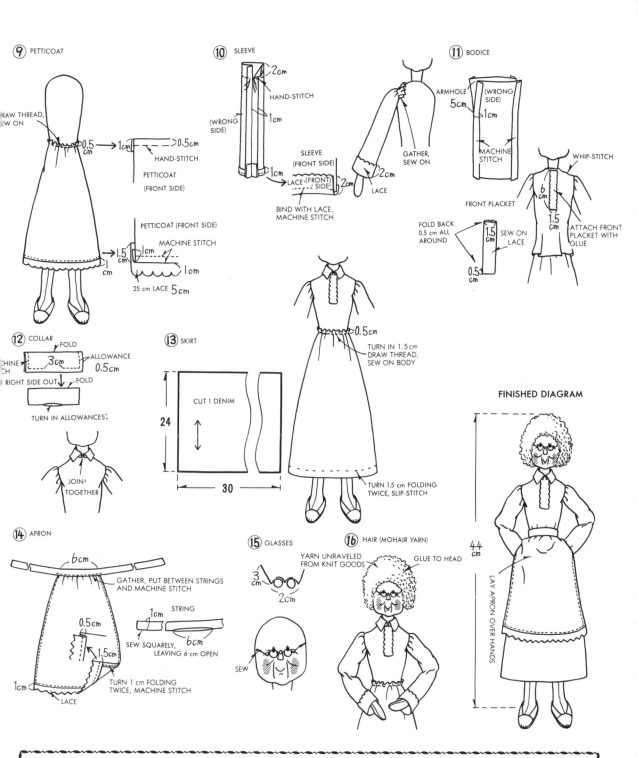

⑨ PETTICOAT

RAW THREAD, SEW ON

0.5 cm → 1cm → 0.5cm
HAND-STITCH

PETTICOAT (FRONT SIDE)

PETTICOAT (FRONT SIDE)

1.5 cm → 1cm
MACHINE STITCH
1cm
1cm
25 cm LACE 5cm

⑩ SLEEVE

2cm
HAND-STITCH
(WRONG SIDE)
1cm
1cm
SLEEVE (FRONT SIDE)
LACE (FRONT SIDE)
2cm
BIND WITH LACE, MACHINE STITCH

GATHER, SEW ON
2cm
LACE

⑪ BODICE

ARMHOLE 5cm
(WRONG SIDE)
1cm
MACHINE STITCH
WHIP-STITCH
FRONT PLACKET
6cm
1.5 cm
ATTACH FRONT PLACKET WITH GLUE
FOLD BACK 0.5 cm ALL AROUND
1.5 cm
SEW ON LACE
0.5 cm

⑫ COLLAR

FOLD
MACHINE STITCH
3cm
ALLOWANCE 0.5 cm
RIGHT SIDE OUT
FOLD
TURN IN ALLOWANCES
JOIN TOGETHER

⑬ SKIRT

CUT 1 DENIM
24
30

0.5cm
TURN IN 1.5 cm DRAW THREAD, SEW ON BODY

TURN 1.5 cm FOLDING TWICE, SLIP-STITCH

FINISHED DIAGRAM

44 cm
LAY APRON OVER HANDS

⑭ APRON

6cm
GATHER, PUT BETWEEN STRINGS AND MACHINE STITCH
0.5 cm
1.5 cm
STRING
1cm
6cm
SEW SQUARELY, LEAVING 6 cm OPEN
1cm
TURN 1 cm FOLDING TWICE, MACHINE STITCH
LACE

⑮ GLASSES

3cm
2cm
SEW

⑯ HAIR (MOHAIR YARN)

YARN UNRAVELED FROM KNIT GOODS
GLUE TO HEAD

MISS BRENDA

Shown on page 35.

The skirt is decorated with white lace attached with shirring. Assembly is basically the same as for Hiji. Make black stockings on her legs by using black georgete as that skin fabric.

YOU'LL NEED:
Head-Foundation, Body, Arms, Legs—86 cm by 58 cm white rayon. Face, Nose, Arms—55 cm by 30 cm beige georgette. Legs—42 cm 35 cm black georgette. Eyes—dacron georgette. Mouth—strands of embroidery thread. Hair—bouclé. Bloomer, Petticoat—82 cm by 29 cm white broadcloth, 50 cm of 2 cm lace. Dress—55 cm by 33.5 cm gingham cheeck, 85 cm by 29 cm gingham smaller check, 630 cm of 2 cm lace ribbon. Shoes—70 cm of 1 cm black braid, 9 cm by 6.5 cm black felt. Also—packing, cotton wadding, polyester batting.

FINISHED SIZE: Refer to diagram.
INSTRUCTIONS:
Make, referring to pages 50-64 for basic method.
Stuff legs firmly with polyester batting.
Sew lace ribbon on the skirt (b), and then shirr it into a piece

55 cm wide.
Stitch shirred lace ribbon to sleeve end, and then sew underarm seam together.
Sew hair all over head in the same manner as shown on page 67.

① PATTERNS (ACTUAL SIZE):

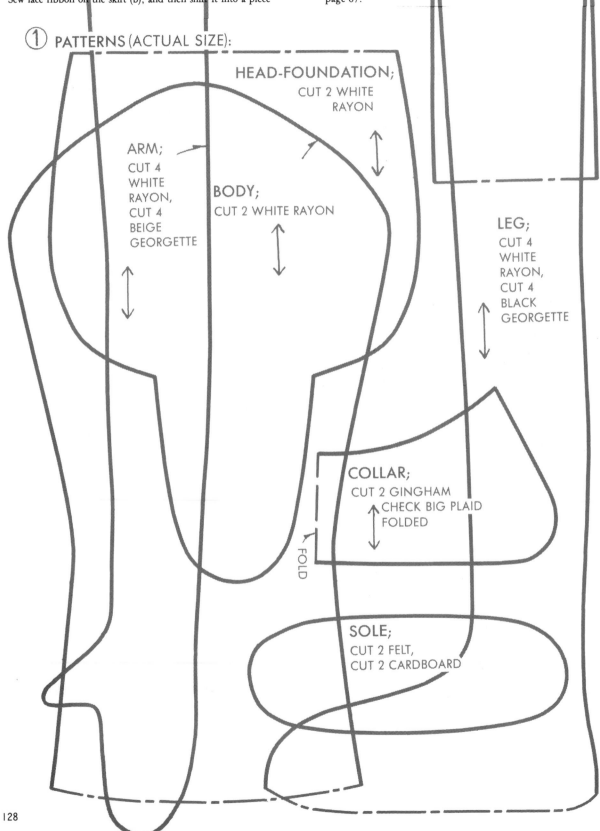

HEAD-FOUNDATION;
CUT 2 WHITE
RAYON

ARM;
CUT 4
WHITE
RAYON,
CUT 4
BEIGE
GEORGETTE

BODY;
CUT 2 WHITE RAYON

LEG;
CUT 4
WHITE
RAYON,
CUT 4
BLACK
GEORGETTE

COLLAR;
CUT 2 GINGHAM
CHECK BIG PLAID
FOLDED

FOLD

SOLE;
CUT 2 FELT,
CUT 2 CARDBOARD

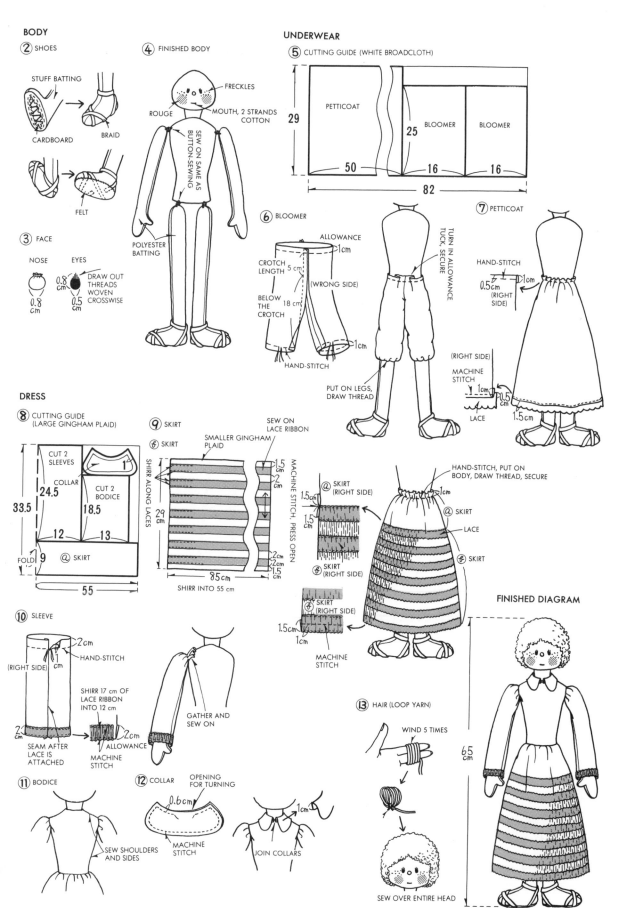

AT HOME ON A RAINY DAY

Shown on page 37.

The way of her legs is special for this doll. Use a fine thread of skin color. Fix her position when making the foundation. Set in head with the face turned slightly sideways.

YOU'LL NEED:
Head-Foundation, Body, Arms, Legs—80 cm by 38 cm white rayon. Face, Nose, Arms, Legs—70 cm by 30 cm cotton jersey. Eyes—dacron georgette. Mouth—strands of embroidery thread. Hair—sport-weight yarn. Kimono—77 cm by 30 cm cotton print. Belt—72 cm by 10 cm broadcloth. Also—No. 18 wire, packing, cotton wadding, polyester batting.
FINISHED SIZE: Refer to diagram.

INSTRUCTIONS:
Referring to pages 50-64 for basic method, make arms and legs in same manner as for Puck, shown on page 117.
Make but with the big toes sewn on top as shown.
Sew kimono, referring to pages 105-106, tie belt round, position her by bending arms and legs.
Sew on hair as shown on page 72.

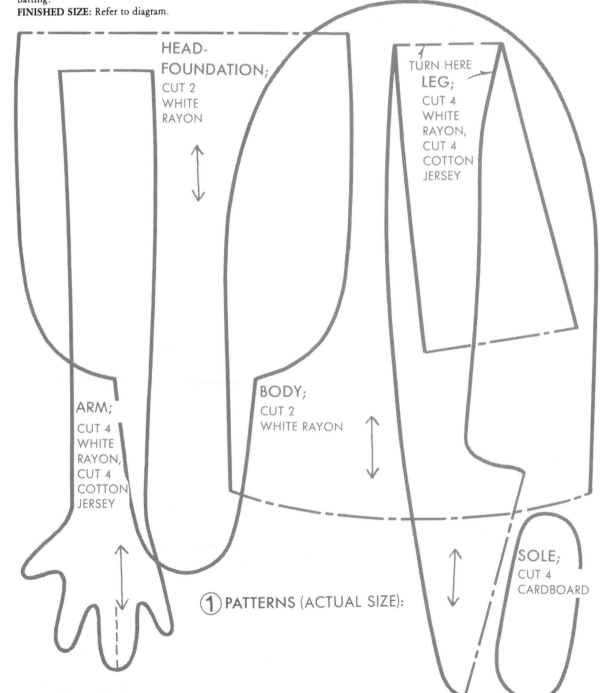

HEAD-FOUNDATION;
CUT 2
WHITE
RAYON

TURN HERE
LEG;
CUT 4
WHITE
RAYON,
CUT 4
COTTON
JERSEY

ARM;
CUT 4
WHITE
RAYON,
CUT 4
COTTON
JERSEY

BODY;
CUT 2
WHITE RAYON

SOLE;
CUT 4
CARDBOARD

① PATTERNS (ACTUAL SIZE):

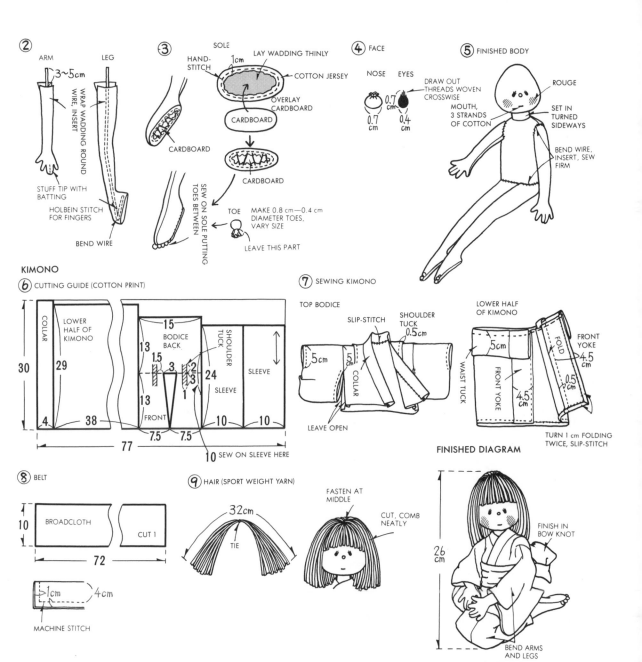

② ARM LEG
3~5cm
WRAP WADDING ROUND WIRE, INSERT
STUFF TIP WITH BATTING
HOLBEIN STITCH FOR FINGERS
BEND WIRE

③ SOLE
HAND-STITCH
1cm
LAY WADDING THINLY
COTTON JERSEY
OVERLAY CARDBOARD
CARDBOARD
CARDBOARD
CARDBOARD
SEW ON SOLE PUTTING TOES BETWEEN
TOE
MAKE 0.8 cm—0.4 cm DIAMETER TOES, VARY SIZE
LEAVE THIS PART

④ FACE
NOSE EYES
0.7 cm 0.7 cm 0.4 cm
0.7 cm
DRAW OUT THREADS WOVEN CROSSWISE
MOUTH, 3 STRANDS OF COTTON

⑤ FINISHED BODY
ROUGE
SET IN TURNED SIDEWAYS
BEND WIRE, INSERT, SEW FIRM

KIMONO

⑥ CUTTING GUIDE (COTTON PRINT)
COLLAR
LOWER HALF OF KIMONO
30
29
4
38
77
15
BODICE BACK
SHOULDER TUCK
13
1.5
3
2
1
13
FRONT
7.5 7.5
24
SLEEVE
SLEEVE
10
10
10
10 SEW ON SLEEVE HERE

⑦ SEWING KIMONO
TOP BODICE
SLIP-STITCH
SHOULDER TUCK 0.5cm
5cm
5
COLLAR
LEAVE OPEN
LOWER HALF OF KIMONO
5cm
WAIST TUCK
FRONT YOKE
FRONT YOKE
FOLD
4.5 cm
0.5 cm
4.5 cm
TURN 1 cm FOLDING TWICE, SLIP-STITCH
FINISHED DIAGRAM

⑧ BELT
10
BROADCLOTH
CUT 1
72
1cm
4cm
MACHINE STITCH

⑨ HAIR (SPORT WEIGHT YARN)
32cm
TIE
FASTEN AT MIDDLE
CUT, COMB NEATLY

26 cm
FINISH IN BOW KNOT
BEND ARMS AND LEGS

RAPUNZEL

Shown on page 38.

This is a very simple cardboard-frame doll. Attach hair of embroidery floss or a bright yellow yarn, combing neatly with a tooth brush or similar tool.

YOU'LL NEED:
Head-Foundation, Body, Arms—60 cm by 13 cm white rayon. Face, Nose, Arms—40 cm by 14 cm cotton jersey. Frame—26 cm by 18 cm cardboard, 35 cm by 20 cm white rayon. Eyes—dacron georgette. Mouth—strands of embroidery thread. Hair—strands of embroidery cotton 3 shades of yellow, floral braid. Petticoat—40 cm by 14 cm white broadcloth, 40 cm of 2 cm lace. Dress—44 cm by 44 cm cotton print, strands of embroidery thread. Apron—12 cm by 11 cm dacron seersucker, 95 cm of 2 cm lace. Also—No. 18 wire, packing, cotton wadding, polyester batting.
FINISHED SIZE: Refer to diagram.

INSTRUCTIONS:
Make according to basic method on pages 50-64. For the way to form and to set in arms, refer to page 110.
Make frame and sew on body. Sew frame cover, lay on the frame as shown.
Lay wadding thinly over the body, sew on bodice and work cross-stitch at center front.
Sew apron on waist, put lace ribbon over it, glue and tie at back.
Make hair by putting 3 shades of embroidery cotton together, fasten in the middle, secure to head. Make hair ornament and attach to the hair.

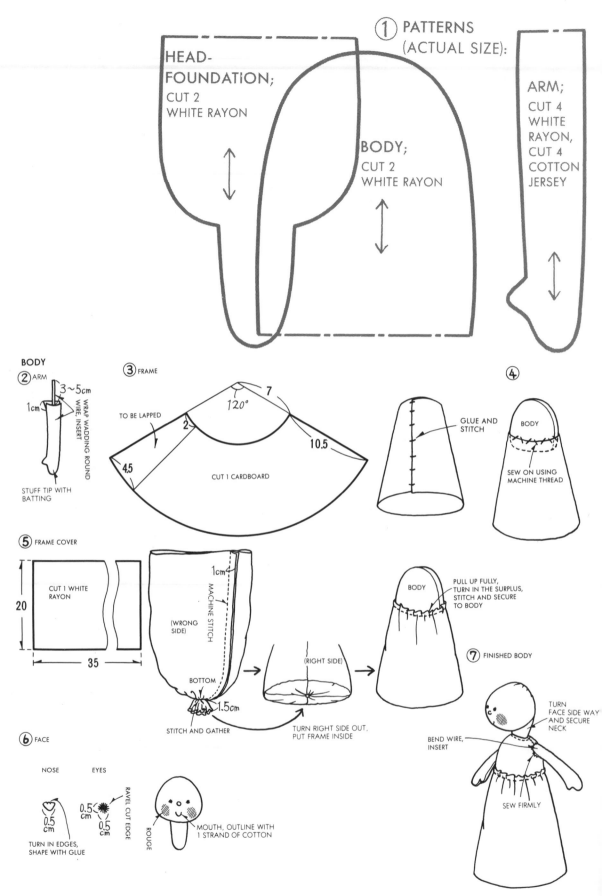

① PATTERNS (ACTUAL SIZE):

HEAD-FOUNDATION; CUT 2 WHITE RAYON

BODY; CUT 2 WHITE RAYON

ARM; CUT 4 WHITE RAYON, CUT 4 COTTON JERSEY

BODY

② ARM

3~5cm
1cm
WRAP WADDING ROUND WIRE, INSERT

STUFF TIP WITH BATTING

③ FRAME

120°
7
TO BE LAPPED
2
10.5
4.5
CUT 1 CARDBOARD

④

GLUE AND STITCH

BODY

SEW ON USING MACHINE THREAD

⑤ FRAME COVER

CUT 1 WHITE RAYON

20

35

1cm
MACHINE STITCH
(WRONG SIDE)

BOTTOM
1.5cm
STITCH AND GATHER

(RIGHT SIDE)

TURN RIGHT SIDE OUT, PUT FRAME INSIDE

BODY
PULL UP FULLY, TURN IN THE SURPLUS, STITCH AND SECURE TO BODY

⑦ FINISHED BODY

⑥ FACE

NOSE

0.5 cm
TURN IN EDGES, SHAPE WITH GLUE

EYES

0.5 cm
RAVEL CUT EDGE
0.5 cm

ROUGE

MOUTH, OUTLINE WITH 1 STRAND OF COTTON

TURN FACE SIDE WAY AND SECURE NECK

BEND WIRE, INSERT

SEW FIRMLY

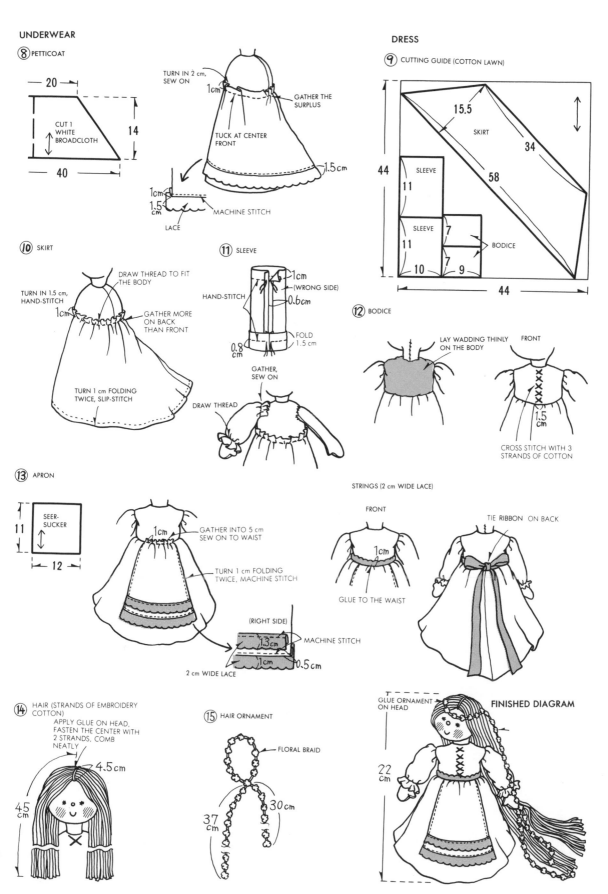

UNDERWEAR

⑧ PETTICOAT

20
CUT 1
WHITE
BROADCLOTH
14
40

TURN IN 2 cm, SEW ON
1cm
GATHER THE SURPLUS
TUCK AT CENTER FRONT
1.5cm
1cm
1.5 cm
MACHINE STITCH
LACE

⑩ SKIRT

DRAW THREAD TO FIT THE BODY
TURN IN 1.5 cm, HAND-STITCH
1cm
GATHER MORE ON BACK THAN FRONT
TURN 1 cm FOLDING TWICE, SLIP-STITCH

⑪ SLEEVE

1cm
(WRONG SIDE)
HAND-STITCH
0.6cm
FOLD 1.5 cm
0.8 cm
GATHER, SEW ON
DRAW THREAD

⑬ APRON

11
SEER-SUCKER
12

1cm
GATHER INTO 5 cm SEW ON TO WAIST
TURN 1 cm FOLDING TWICE, MACHINE STITCH
(RIGHT SIDE)
1.3cm
MACHINE STITCH
1cm
0.5 cm
2 cm WIDE LACE

⑭ HAIR (STRANDS OF EMBROIDERY COTTON)

APPLY GLUE ON HEAD, FASTEN THE CENTER WITH 2 STRANDS, COMB NEATLY
4.5cm
45 cm

⑮ HAIR ORNAMENT

FLORAL BRAID
30 cm
37 cm

DRESS

⑨ CUTTING GUIDE (COTTON LAWN)

15.5
SKIRT
34
44
SLEEVE
11
58
SLEEVE
11
7
BODICE
10
7
9
44

⑫ BODICE

LAY WADDING THINLY ON THE BODY
FRONT
1.5 cm
CROSS STITCH WITH 3 STRANDS OF COTTON

STRINGS (2 cm WIDE LACE)

FRONT
1cm
GLUE TO THE WAIST
TIE RIBBON ON BACK

GLUE ORNAMENT ON HEAD
FINISHED DIAGRAM
22 cm

133

PRINCESS ELISSA

Shown on page 39.

Use thick cardboard for the frame if it is availabe. Make the doll most princesslike, using gorgeous fabrics and fancy ribbons.

YOU'LL NEED:

Head-Foundation, Body, Arms—45 cm by 23 cm white rayon. Face, Nose, Arms—30 cm by 22 cm georgette. Frame—33 cm by 33 cm cardboard, 40 cm by 35 cm white rayon. Eyes—dacron georgette. Mouth—strands of embroidery thread. Hair—strands embroidery thread, 210 cm of 3.5 cm lace ribbon, artificial flower. Petticoat—55 cm by 29 cm non-woven fabric. Dress—90 cm by 51 cm lace fabric, 90 cm by 44cm pink lining, 130 cm of 3.5 cm lace ribbon, artificial flower. Also—No. 18 wire, packing, cotton wadding, polyester batting.
FINISHED SIZE: Refer to diagram.

INSTRUCTIONS:

Referring to pages 50-64 for basic method, make arms in same manner as for Lost Angels on page 110; make frame as shown on page 132.
Lay wadding on the body in same manner as for Rapunzel on page 132; sew on bodice with the lining beneath. Sew skirt and then its lining securing 2 pieces together at waist. Decorate front of neck and apply flowers on the skirt.
Position her with the arm bent, glue sleeve ends together.

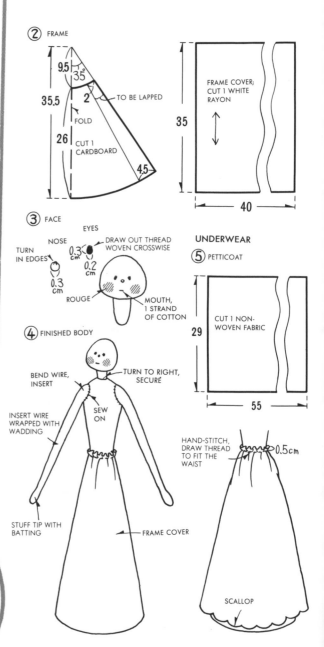

① PATTERNS (ACTUAL SIZE):

ARM;
CUT 4 WHITE RAYON, CUT 4 COTTON JERSEY

HEAD-FOUNDATION; CUT 2 WHITE RAYON

BODY; CUT 2 WHITE RAYON

② FRAME

9.5
35°
35.5
2
TO BE LAPPED
FOLD
26
CUT 1 CARDBOARD
45

FRAME COVER; CUT 1 WHITE RAYON
35
40

③ FACE

EYES
NOSE
DRAW OUT THREAD WOVEN CROSSWISE
TURN IN EDGES
0.3 cm
0.2 cm
0.3 cm
ROUGE
MOUTH, 1 STRAND OF COTTON

④ FINISHED BODY

BEND WIRE, INSERT
TURN TO RIGHT, SECURE
INSERT WIRE WRAPPED WITH WADDING
SEW ON
STUFF TIP WITH BATTING
FRAME COVER

UNDERWEAR

⑤ PETTICOAT

CUT 1 NON-WOVEN FABRIC
29
55

HAND-STITCH, DRAW THREAD TO FIT THE WAIST
0.5cm
SCALLOP

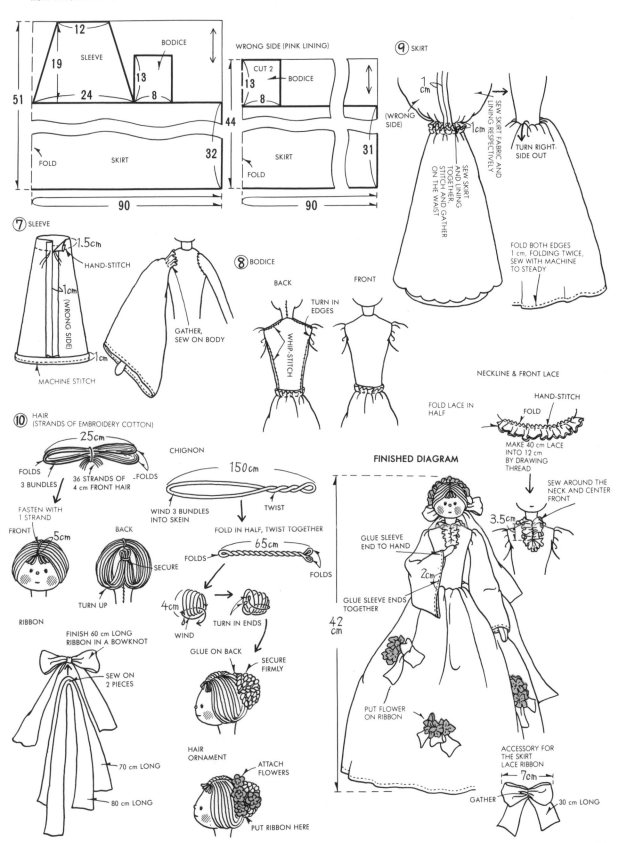

ROYAL PRINCESS OF THE STARS

Shown on page 40.

If a star-print fabric is not available, make her the princess of your own choice, such as apples, flowers, or birds. Make her face somewhat smaller than its size.

YOU'LL NEED:
Head-Foundation, Body, Arms, Legs—70 cm by 28 cm white rayon. Face, Nose, Arms, Legs—50 cm by 28 cm cotton jersey. Eyes—dacron georgette. Mouth—strands of embroidery thread. Hair—strands of embroidery thread, 13 cm of 2.5 cm broadcloth. Bloomer, Petticoat—85 cm by 26 cm white georgette. Dress, Veil—90 cm by 85 cm dacron print, 72 cm by 37 cm silver lamé, 62 cm of 2.5 cm braid. Also—packing, cotton wadding, polyester batting.
FINISHED SIZE: Refer to diagram.

INSTRUCTIONS:
Make by referring to Hiji on pages 50-64 for basic method.
Stuff polyester batting firmly into arms and legs. Before the bodice is sewn on, lay wadding thinly over the body. Make collar by gathering braid and stitch to position.
Put silver lamé on wrong side of veil, securing with slip-stitch.
Sew on hair, put veil over, secure with slip-stitch. Put crown on top.

① PATTERNS (ACTUAL SIZE):

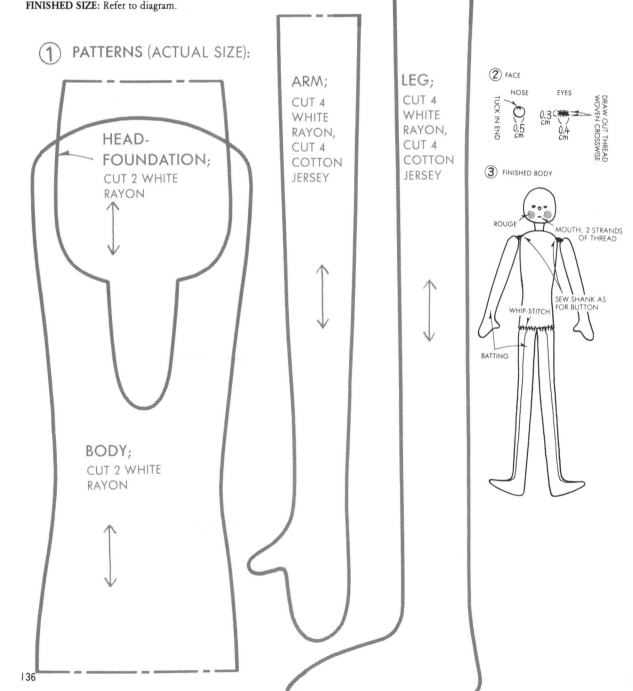

HEAD-FOUNDATION;
CUT 2 WHITE RAYON

BODY;
CUT 2 WHITE RAYON

ARM;
CUT 4 WHITE RAYON, CUT 4 COTTON JERSEY

LEG;
CUT 4 WHITE RAYON, CUT 4 COTTON JERSEY

② FACE

TUCK IN END

NOSE
0.5 cm

EYES
0.3 cm
0.4 cm

DRAW OUT THREAD WOVEN CROSSWISE

③ FINISHED BODY

ROUGE

MOUTH, 2 STRANDS OF THREAD

SEW SHANK AS FOR BUTTON

WHIP-STITCH

BATTING

DRESS, VEIL, UNDERWEAR

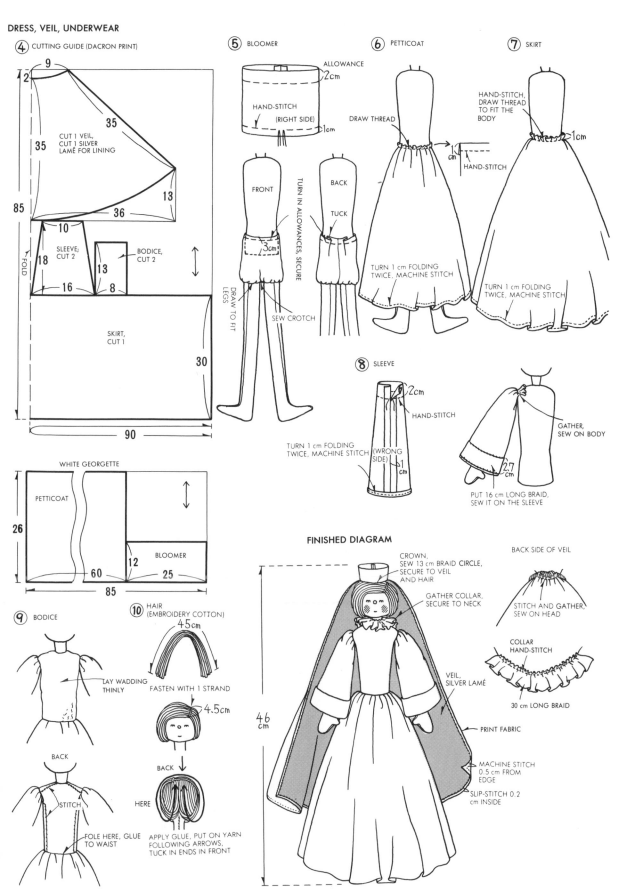

④ CUTTING GUIDE (DACRON PRINT)

9
2

35
35
36
13

CUT 1 VEIL,
CUT 1 SILVER
LAMÉ FOR LINING

85

10
SLEEVE;
CUT 2
18
16
8
13

BODICE,
CUT 2

FOLD

SKIRT,
CUT 1

30

90

WHITE GEORGETTE

PETTICOAT

26

BLOOMER

60
12
25
85

⑤ BLOOMER

ALLOWANCE
2cm

HAND-STITCH
(RIGHT SIDE)
1cm

FRONT
BACK
TUCK

3cm

TURN IN ALLOWANCES, SECURE

DRAW TO FIT LEGS

SEW CROTCH

⑥ PETTICOAT

DRAW THREAD

1 cm
HAND-STITCH

TURN 1 cm FOLDING
TWICE, MACHINE STITCH

⑦ SKIRT

HAND-STITCH,
DRAW THREAD
TO FIT THE
BODY

1cm

TURN 1 cm FOLDING
TWICE, MACHINE STITCH

⑧ SLEEVE

2cm
HAND-STITCH

TURN 1 cm FOLDING
TWICE, MACHINE STITCH (WRONG SIDE)
1 cm

GATHER,
SEW ON BODY

2.7 cm

PUT 16 cm LONG BRAID,
SEW IT ON THE SLEEVE

FINISHED DIAGRAM

CROWN,
SEW 13 cm BRAID CIRCLE,
SECURE TO VEIL
AND HAIR

GATHER COLLAR,
SECURE TO NECK

VEIL,
SILVER LAMÉ

PRINT FABRIC

MACHINE STITCH
0.5 cm FROM
EDGE

SLIP-STITCH 0.2
cm INSIDE

46 cm

BACK SIDE OF VEIL

STITCH AND GATHER,
SEW ON HEAD

COLLAR
HAND-STITCH

30 cm LONG BRAID

⑨ BODICE

LAY WADDING
THINLY

BACK

STITCH

FOLE HERE, GLUE
TO WAIST

⑩ HAIR
(EMBROIDERY COTTON)

45cm

FASTEN WITH 1 STRAND

4.5cm

BACK

HERE

APPLY GLUE, PUT ON YARN
FOLLOWING ARROWS,
TUCK IN ENDS IN FRONT

MADAM LILAS

Shown on page 41.

Stuff packing in carefully to give a smooth finish to the front part of the neck. Note the level of chignon in back. Finish the hair and dress in shades of lilac.

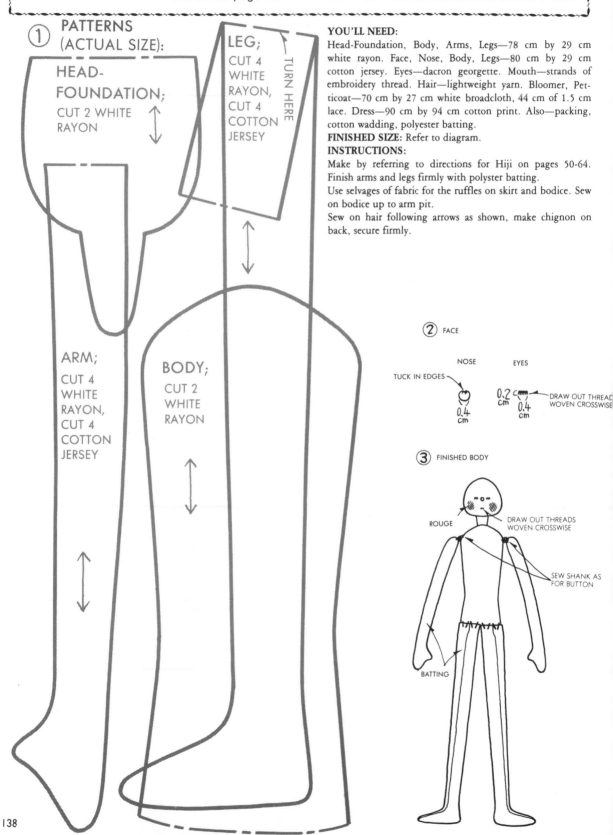

① PATTERNS (ACTUAL SIZE):

HEAD-FOUNDATION;
CUT 2 WHITE RAYON

LEG;
CUT 4 WHITE RAYON,
CUT 4 COTTON JERSEY

TURN HERE

ARM;
CUT 4 WHITE RAYON,
CUT 4 COTTON JERSEY

BODY;
CUT 2 WHITE RAYON

YOU'LL NEED:
Head-Foundation, Body, Arms, Legs—78 cm by 29 cm white rayon. Face, Nose, Body, Legs—80 cm by 29 cm cotton jersey. Eyes—dacron georgette. Mouth—strands of embroidery thread. Hair—lightweight yarn. Bloomer, Petticoat—70 cm by 27 cm white broadcloth, 44 cm of 1.5 cm lace. Dress—90 cm by 94 cm cotton print. Also—packing, cotton wadding, polyester batting.

FINISHED SIZE: Refer to diagram.

INSTRUCTIONS:
Make by referring to directions for Hiji on pages 50-64. Finish arms and legs firmly with polyster batting.
Use selvages of fabric for the ruffles on skirt and bodice. Sew on bodice up to arm pit.
Sew on hair following arrows as shown, make chignon on back, secure firmly.

② FACE

NOSE

TUCK IN EDGES

0.4 cm

EYES

0.2 cm   0.4 cm

DRAW OUT THREAD WOVEN CROSSWISE

③ FINISHED BODY

ROUGE

DRAW OUT THREADS WOVEN CROSSWISE

SEW SHANK AS FOR BUTTON

BATTING

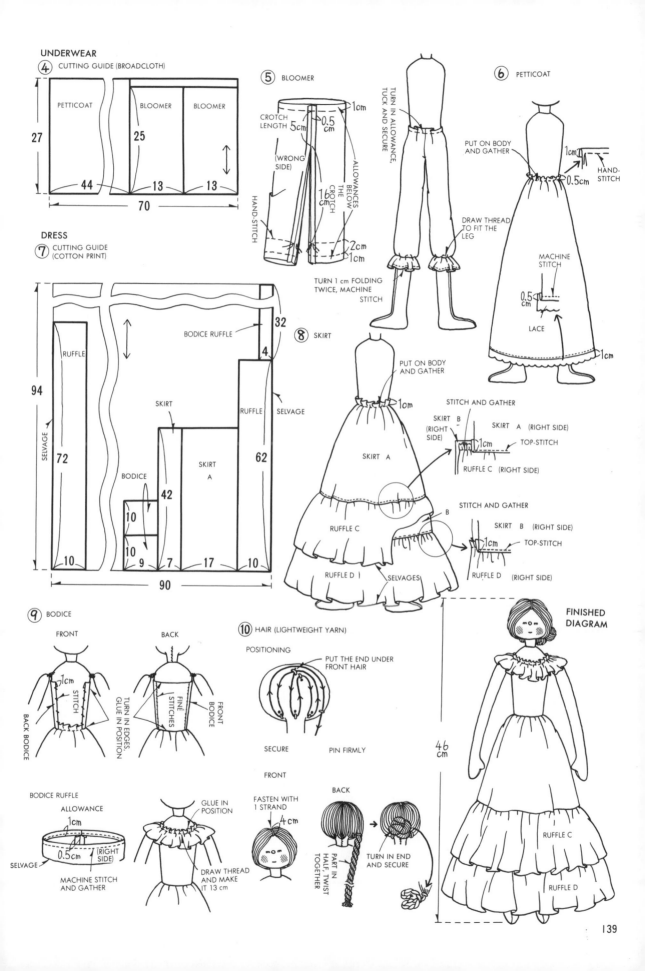

UNDERWEAR

④ CUTTING GUIDE (BROADCLOTH)

PETTICOAT

BLOOMER

BLOOMER

27

25

44   13   13

70

⑤ BLOOMER

1cm

CROTCH
LENGTH 5cm   0.5 cm

(WRONG SIDE)

16 cm

ALLOWANCES BELOW THE CROTCH

HAND-STITCH

2cm
1cm

TURN 1 cm FOLDING
TWICE, MACHINE
STITCH

TURN IN ALLOWANCE,
TUCK AND SECURE

DRAW THREAD
TO FIT THE
LEG

⑥ PETTICOAT

PUT ON BODY
AND GATHER

1cm

0.5cm

HAND-STITCH

MACHINE
STITCH

0.5 cm

LACE

1cm

DRESS

⑦ CUTTING GUIDE
(COTTON PRINT)

RUFFLE

94

SELVAGE

72

BODICE

SKIRT

BODICE RUFFLE

32

4

RUFFLE

62

SELVAGE

42

10

10

10

9   7   17   10

90

⑧ SKIRT

PUT ON BODY
AND GATHER

1cm

SKIRT A

RUFFLE C

RUFFLE D

SELVAGES

STITCH AND GATHER

SKIRT B
(RIGHT SIDE)

SKIRT A (RIGHT SIDE)

1cm

TOP-STITCH

RUFFLE C (RIGHT SIDE)

STITCH AND GATHER

B

SKIRT B (RIGHT SIDE)

1cm

TOP-STITCH

RUFFLE D (RIGHT SIDE)

⑨ BODICE

FRONT

BACK

1cm

STITCH

BACK BODICE

TURN IN EDGES,
GLUE IN POSITION

FINE STITCHES

FRONT BODICE

BODICE RUFFLE

ALLOWANCE

1cm

0.5cm   (RIGHT SIDE)

SELVAGE

MACHINE STITCH
AND GATHER

GLUE IN
POSITION

DRAW THREAD
AND MAKE
IT 13 cm

⑩ HAIR (LIGHTWEIGHT YARN)

POSITIONING

PUT THE END UNDER
FRONT HAIR

SECURE   PIN FIRMLY

FRONT

FASTEN WITH
1 STRAND

4cm

BACK

PART IN
HALF, TWIST
TOGETHER

TURN IN END
AND SECURE

FINISHED
DIAGRAM

46 cm

RUFFLE C

RUFFLE D

139

JOHN & BARBARA

Shown on page 42.

The twins are made in the same way. Simply make one a boy and the other a girl, disigning their face and legs differently. Make dresses with a soft fabric in a pale color.

YOU'LL NEED:
Head-Foundation, Body, Arms, Legs—45 cm by 23 cm white rayon. Face, Nose, Arms, Legs—40 cm by 20 cm beige cotton jersey. Eyes—dacron georgette. Mouth—strands of embroidery thread. Hair—mohair yarn. Dress, Cap, Bloomer—40 cm by 26 cm crepe, 40 cm of 0.6 cm ribbon, 50 cm of 2.5 cm lace. Also—packing, cotton wadding, polyster batting.

FINISHED SIZE: Refer to diagram.
INSTRUCTIONS:
Make according to the directions for Hiji shown on pages 50-64. Make hair, winding yarn round fingers, and sew all over head without snipping the yarn between curls.

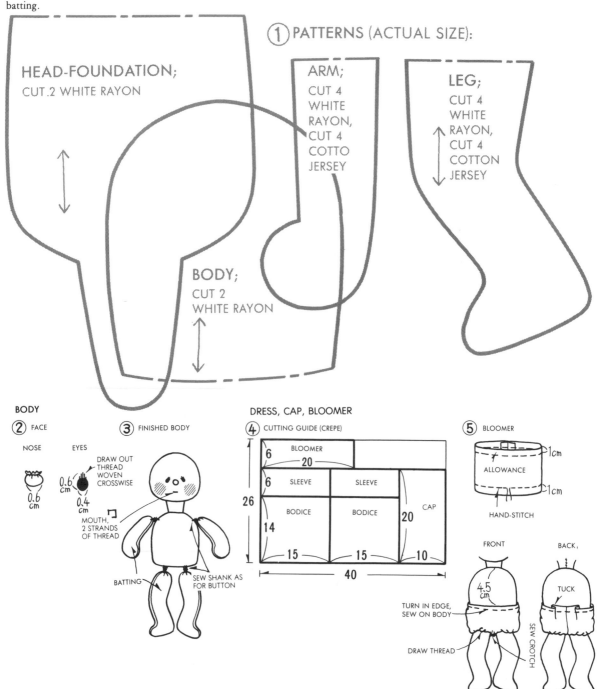

① PATTERNS (ACTUAL SIZE):

HEAD-FOUNDATION;
CUT 2 WHITE RAYON

ARM;
CUT 4 WHITE RAYON,
CUT 4 COTTO JERSEY

LEG;
CUT 4 WHITE RAYON,
CUT 4 COTTON JERSEY

BODY;
CUT 2 WHITE RAYON

BODY

② FACE

NOSE
0.6 cm

EYES
0.6 cm
0.4 cm
DRAW OUT THREAD WOVEN CROSSWISE

MOUTH, 2 STRANDS OF THREAD

③ FINISHED BODY

BATTING

SEW SHANK AS FOR BUTTON

DRESS, CAP, BLOOMER

④ CUTTING GUIDE (CREPE)

6 BLOOMER — 20 —
6 SLEEVE | SLEEVE
26 | 14 | BODICE | BODICE | CAP 20
— 15 — | — 15 — | — 10 —
— 40 —

⑤ BLOOMER
1cm
ALLOWANCE
1cm
HAND-STITCH

FRONT
4.5 cm
TURN IN EDGE, SEW ON BODY
DRAW THREAD

BACK,
TUCK
SEW CROTCH

140

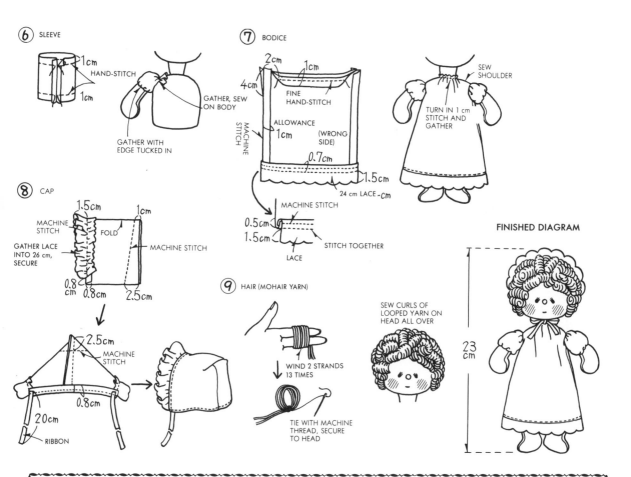

⑥ SLEEVE

1cm
HAND-STITCH
1cm

GATHER WITH
EDGE TUCKED IN

GATHER, SEW
ON BODY

⑦ BODICE

2cm
1cm
4cm

FINE
HAND-STITCH

MACHINE STITCH

ALLOWANCE
1cm
(WRONG
SIDE)

0.7cm

1.5cm

24 cm LACE -cm

SEW SHOULDER

TURN IN 1 cm
STITCH AND
GATHER

0.5cm
1.5cm

MACHINE STITCH

STITCH TOGETHER

LACE

⑧ CAP

1.5cm
1cm

MACHINE STITCH
FOLD
MACHINE STITCH

GATHER LACE
INTO 26 cm,
SECURE

0.8cm
0.8cm
2.5cm

2.5cm
MACHINE STITCH

0.8cm

20cm

RIBBON

⑨ HAIR (MOHAIR YARN)

WIND 2 STRANDS
13 TIMES

TIE WITH MACHINE
THREAD, SECURE
TO HEAD

SEW CURLS OF
LOOPED YARN ON
HEAD ALL OVER

FINISHED DIAGRAM

23 cm

MIMI & LULU & POPO

Shown on page 43.

Make these all in the same manner, using an easy-to-handle sheer fabric like lawn. Mark the different individuals with their dresses.

YOU'LL NEED (for each):
Head-Foundation, Body, Arms, Legs—40 cm by 27 cm white rayon. Face, Nose, Arms, Legs—50 cm by 15 cm beige georgette. Eyes—dacron georgette. Mouth —strands of embroidery thread. Hair— frizzle yarn, 20 cm of 0.3 cm ribbon. Bloomer—20 cm by 10 cm white broad-cloth. Petticoat—60 cm of 5 cm lace. Dress, Cap—50 cm by 25.5 cm lawn, 28 cm of 1.5 cm lace. Also—packing, cotton wadding, polyester batting.
FINISHED SIZE: Refer to diagram.
INSTRUCTIONS:
Make according to the method on pages 50-64.
Sew on hair in same manner as shown on page 72.
Make each in the same way and clothe in dresses of different color.

① PATTERNS (ACTUAL SIZE):

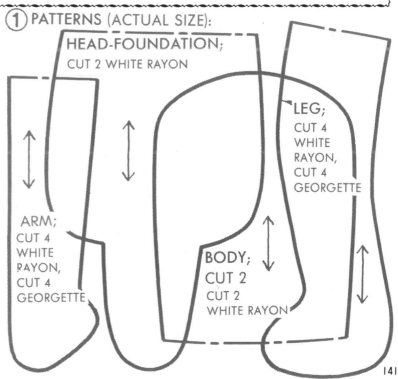

HEAD-FOUNDATION;
CUT 2 WHITE RAYON

LEG;
CUT 4
WHITE
RAYON,
CUT 4
GEORGETTE

ARM;
CUT 4
WHITE
RAYON,
CUT 4
GEORGETTE

BODY;
CUT 2
CUT 2
WHITE RAYON

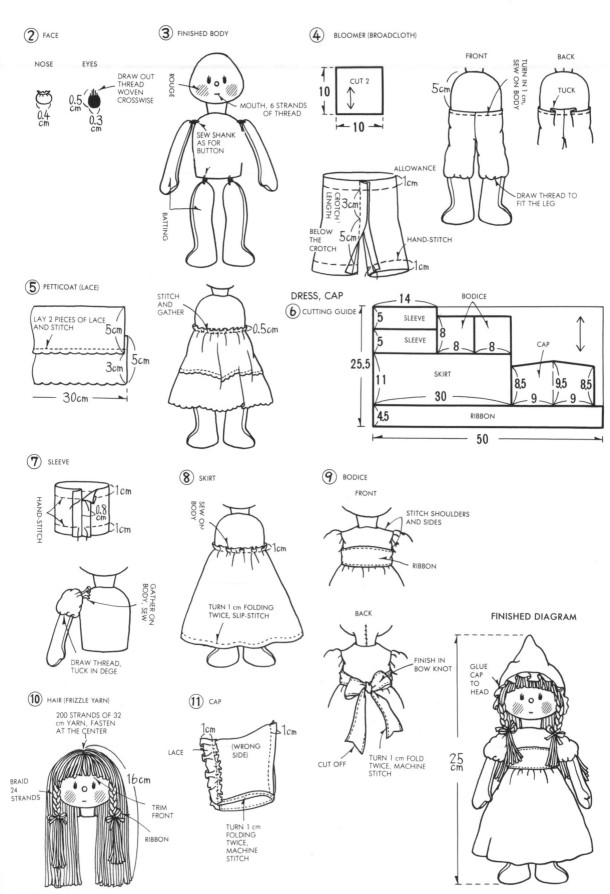

PRINCESS FROM THE LAND OF BAMBOO

Shown on page 44.

These are very simply made. Make them stand by putting a felt piece over the cardboard base. Make the grandparents' features by referring to the picture.

YOU'LL NEED (for each):

Head-Foundation—9 cm by 15 cm white rayon. Face, Nose —20 cm by 20 cm beige georgette. Eyes—dacron georgette. Mouth—strands of embroidery thread. Body—6.5 cm by 13 cm cardboard. Also—packing, cotton wadding, polyester batting.

(Princess): Kimono—17 cm by 6.5 cm each, light pink, rose felt. Collar—17 cm by 3 cm each, white, purple felt. Hair—sport-weight yarn. Ribbon—strands of cotton small amount each, yellow brown, pink.

(Grandma): Kimono—6.5 cm by 17 cm dark blue felt. Collar—17 cm by 3 cm each, white, gray felt. Wrinkles— silk thread. Hair—worsted-weight yarn.

(Grandpa): Kimono—6.5 cm by 17 cm dark green felt. Collar—17 cm by 3 cm each, white, brown felt. Wrinkles— silk thread. Hair—worsted-weight yarn.

FINISHED SIZE: Refer to diagram.

INSTRUCTIONS:

Make heads and faces according to directions for Hiji on pages 50-64. Make grandpa's face long lengthwise. Put a little rounded wadding on the faces of both grandparents right above the mouths. Draw the thread of sewn wrinkles to make their facial features.

① PATTERNS (ACTUAL SIZE):

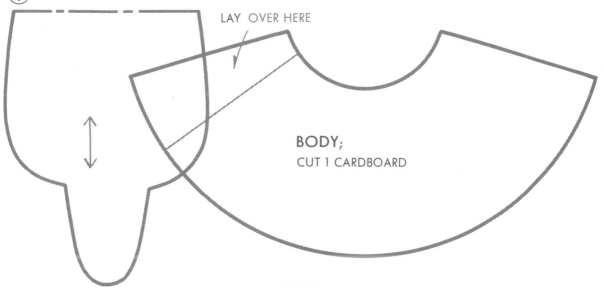

LAY OVER HERE

BODY;
CUT 1 CARDBOARD

KIMONO;
CUT 1 EACH, FELT PINK,
ROSE FOR PRINCESS,
DARK BLUE FOR GRANDMA,
DARK GREEN FOR GRANDPA

CUT 1 EACH, FELT WHITE,
PURPLE FOR PRINCESS,
WHITE, GRAY FOR GRANDMA,
DARK GREEN FOR GRANDPA

COLLAR; CUT 1 EACH, FELT
WHITE, PURPLE FOR PRINCESS, WHITE, GRAY FOR GRANDMA, DARK GREEN FOR GRANDPA

(PRINCESS)

2 FACE

NOSE
EYES

DRAW OUT THREAD WOVEN CROSSWISE

0.5 cm

0.5 cm
0.3 cm

3 BODY

GLUE AND STITCH

4 FINISHED BODY

ROUGE

MOUTH, 2 STRANDS OF COTTON

APPLY GLUE ON NECK, INSERT

5 KIMONO

COLLAR

KIMONO

WHITE

PURPLE

OVERLAY WHITE, PURPLE IN TURN, GLUE FIRMLY

PINK

ROSE

SECURE AT INSIDE

6 HAIR (SPORT YARN)

22 cm

200 THREADS

FASTEN

TIE IN THE MIDDLE

APPLY GLUE, ATTACH, COMB NEATLY

TIE 10 STRANDS TOGETHER WITH 6 STRANDS OF EMBROIDERY COTTON YELLOW BROWN, PINK

3 cm

FINISHED DIAGRAM

13.5 cm

(GRANDPA, GRANDMA)

1 FACE

WRINKLES
SILK 1 STRAND

14 OUT
12 13 2 OUT 1 IN
10 9 11 4 3 IN
6 5
8 7

PUT ON ROUNDED WADDING, COVER WITH SKIN FABRIC

NOSE

EYES

0.7 cm

0.5 cm
0.3 cm

DRAW OUT THREAD WOVEN CROSSWISE

2 HAIR (WORSTED YARN)

(GRANDPA)

14 cm

TIE 30 STRANDS TOGETHER IN THE MIDDLE, SECURE TO HEAD

SPREAD EVENLY

PASS YARN AROUND, SECURE WITH MACHINE THREAD

FASTEN WITH THE END TUCKED IN

FASTEN

SEW ON

PUT THE YARN UPWARD, TIE WITH YARN AND SECURE

BULGE

FINISHED DIAGRAM

(GRANDPA)

15.5 cm

WHITE

BROWN

DARK GREEN

ATTACH EYES ON THE WRINKLES

ROUGE

MOUTH, 2 STRANDS OF COTTON

(GRANDMA)

40 STRANDS OF 32 cm BUNDLE

FASTEN AT THE MIDDLE, SECURE

BACK

GLUE, COMB NEATLY

4.5 cm

FASTEN

(GRANDMA)

12.5 cm

WHITE

GRAY

DARK BLUE

144

GLOWING SUNSET

Shown on page 45.

Noses are very tiny, as you see in the picture. Attach skin fabric cut to nose size in its position. For fabric, try to use one of most Japaneselike patterns.

YOU'LL NEED (for each):

Head-Foundation—8 cm by 12 cm white rayon. Body, Collar —14 cm by 9 cm cotton fabric. Face, Nose—10 cm by 10 cm beige georgette. Eyes—dacron georgette. Mouth—strands of embroidery thread. Hair—sport-weight yarn. Also—packing, cotton wadding, polyester batting.

FINISHED SIZE: Refer to diagram.

INSTRUCTIONS:

Make by referring to pages 50-64 for the basic method.

Seam body along the pattern and cut out, leaving a little allowance all around; turn right side out and stuff packing firmly.

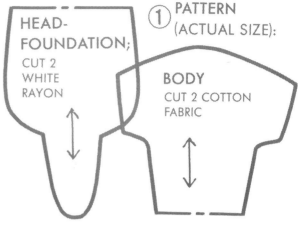

(1) PATTERN (ACTUAL SIZE):

HEAD-FOUNDATION; CUT 2 WHITE RAYON

BODY CUT 2 COTTON FABRIC

(2) FACE

NOSE — 0.3 cm

EYES — 0.4 cm, 0.3 cm — DRAW OUT THREAD WOVEN CROSSWISE

(3) BODY

STUFF PACKING

ROUGE

MOUTH, 2 STRANDS OF COTTON

APPLY GLUE INSIDE NECK HOLE, INSERT NECK

WHIP-STITCH

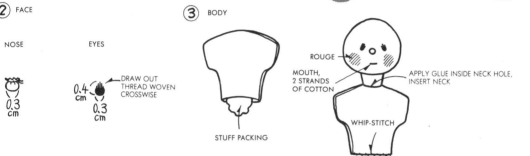

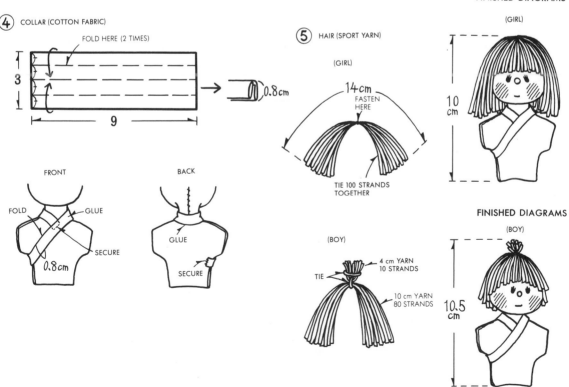

(4) COLLAR (COTTON FABRIC)

FOLD HERE (2 TIMES)

3 — 9 — 0.8cm

FRONT

FOLD — GLUE

SECURE

0.8cm

BACK

GLUE

SECURE

(5) HAIR (SPORT YARN)

(GIRL)

14cm FASTEN HERE

TIE 100 STRANDS TOGETHER

(BOY)

TIE

4 cm YARN 10 STRANDS

10 cm YARN 80 STRANDS

FINISHED DIAGRAMS

(GIRL)

10 cm

FINISHED DIAGRAMS

(BOY)

10.5 cm

MITCHI

Shown on page 46.

Though she is very tall, she is very simple to make. Her voluminous skirt is designed to keep things indide, so secure the waist firmly to the body.

YOU'LL NEED:
Head-Foundation, Body, Arms—50 cm by 40 cm white rayon. Face, Noes, Arms—45 cm by 30 cm cotton jersey. Body—34 cm by 16 cm corduroy. Eyes—dacron georgette. Mouth—strands of embroidery thread. Hair—lightweight yarn. Sleeves, Skirt, Hood—90 cm by 80 cm velveteen, 90 cm of 3 cm lace, 80 cm of 0.7 cm velvet ribbon. In-Pocket— 90 cm by 47 cm white rayon. Also—packing, cotton wadding, polyester batting.

FINISHED SIZE: Refer to diagram.

INSTRUCTIONS:
Make by referring to pages 54-64 for the basic method. Machine stitch the corduroy body laid over the white rayon. Sew pocket on the skirt, make an opening at center back.

1 PATTERNS (ACTUAL SIZE):

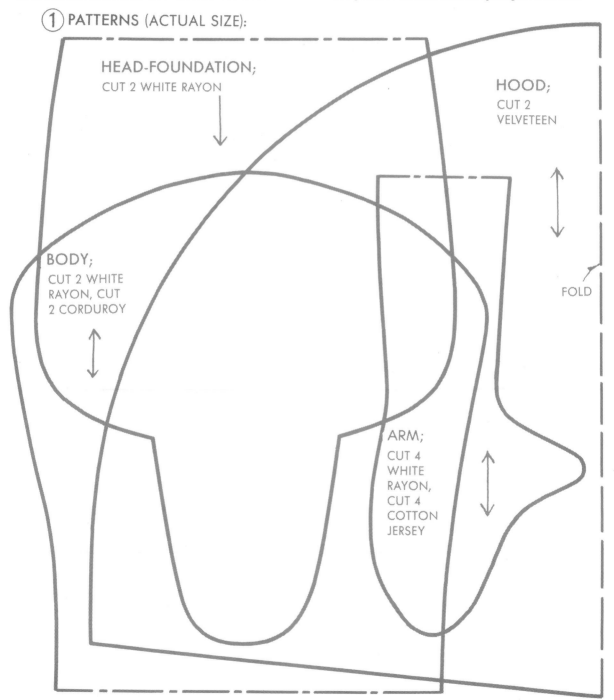

HEAD-FOUNDATION;
CUT 2 WHITE RAYON

HOOD;
CUT 2
VELVETEEN

FOLD

BODY;
CUT 2 WHITE
RAYON, CUT
2 CORDUROY

ARM;
CUT 4
WHITE
RAYON,
CUT 4
COTTON
JERSEY

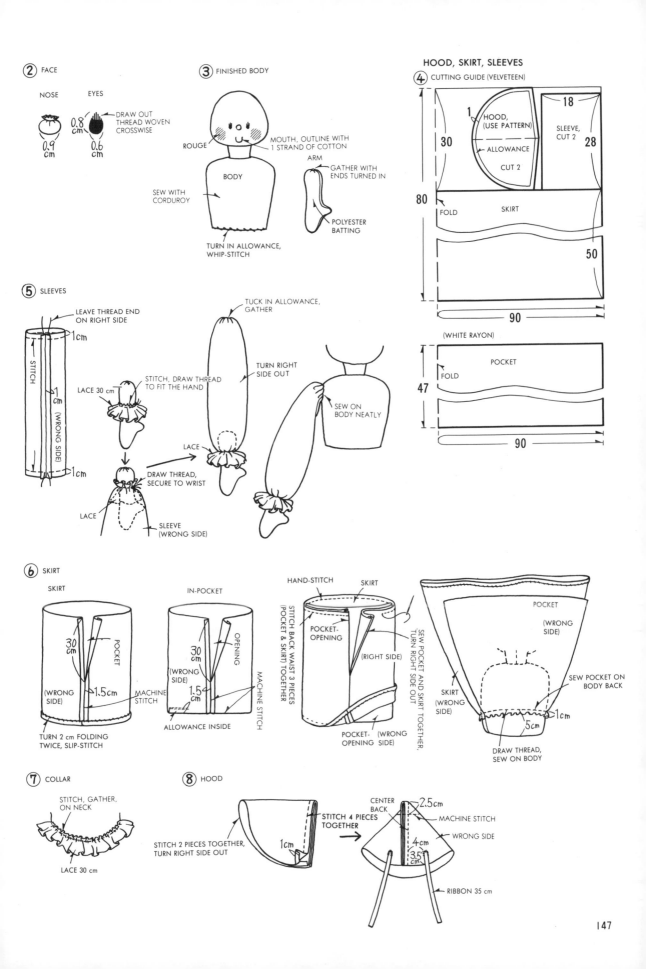

② FACE

NOSE

0.9 cm

EYES

0.8 cm
0.6 cm

DRAW OUT THREAD WOVEN CROSSWISE

③ FINISHED BODY

ROUGE

BODY

SEW WITH CORDUROY

MOUTH, OUTLINE WITH 1 STRAND OF COTTON

TURN IN ALLOWANCE, WHIP-STITCH

ARM

GATHER WITH ENDS TURNED IN

POLYESTER BATTING

HOOD, SKIRT, SLEEVES

④ CUTTING GUIDE (VELVETEEN)

1
HOOD, (USE PATTERN)
ALLOWANCE
CUT 2

18
SLEEVE, CUT 2
28

30

80

FOLD
SKIRT

50

90

(WHITE RAYON)

POCKET

FOLD

47

90

⑤ SLEEVES

LEAVE THREAD END ON RIGHT SIDE

1cm

STITCH

1 cm

(WRONG SIDE)

1cm

LACE 30 cm

STITCH, DRAW THREAD TO FIT THE HAND

LACE

DRAW THREAD, SECURE TO WRIST

SLEEVE (WRONG SIDE)

TUCK IN ALLOWANCE, GATHER

TURN RIGHT SIDE OUT

LACE

SEW ON BODY NEATLY

⑥ SKIRT

SKIRT

30 cm
1.5cm

(WRONG SIDE)

POCKET

MACHINE STITCH

TURN 2 cm FOLDING TWICE, SLIP-STITCH

IN-POCKET

30 cm

(WRONG SIDE)

1.5 cm

OPENING

MACHINE STITCH

ALLOWANCE INSIDE

HAND-STITCH

SKIRT

POCKET-OPENING

(RIGHT SIDE)

STITCH BACK WAIST 3 PIECES (POCKET & SKIRT) TOGETHER

POCKET-OPENING SIDE)

(WRONG

SEW POCKET AND SKIRT TOGETHER, TURN RIGHT SIDE OUT

POCKET

(WRONG SIDE)

SKIRT (WRONG SIDE)

SEW POCKET ON BODY BACK

5cm
1cm

DRAW THREAD, SEW ON BODY

⑦ COLLAR

STITCH, GATHER, ON NECK

LACE 30 cm

⑧ HOOD

STITCH 2 PIECES TOGETHER, TURN RIGHT SIDE OUT

1cm

CENTER BACK

STITCH 4 PIECES TOGETHER

2.5cm

MACHINE STITCH

WRONG SIDE

4cm
3.5cm

RIBBON 35 cm

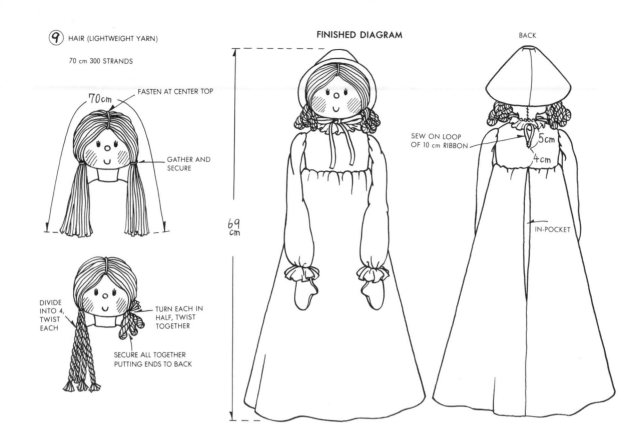

⑨ HAIR (LIGHTWEIGHT YARN)

70 cm 300 STRANDS

70cm

FASTEN AT CENTER TOP

GATHER AND SECURE

DIVIDE INTO 4, TWIST EACH

TURN EACH IN HALF, TWIST TOGETHER

SECURE ALL TOGETHER PUTTING ENDS TO BACK

69 cm

BACK

SEW ON LOOP OF 10 cm RIBBON

5cm

4cm

IN-POCKET

ROMMY & DORON

Shown on page 47.

Those are long bodied dolls with short legs. Stuff the body carefully to give a smooth finish. Make them marionettes, and enjoy talking and manipulating them.

YOU'LL NEED:

(Rommy): Head-Foundation, Arms, Legs—76 cm by 26 cm white rayon. Face, Nose, Arms, Legs—66 cm by 26 cm beige cotton jersey. Eyes—dacron georgette. Mouth—strands of embroidery thread. Hair—pink, blue, worsted yarn, No. 30 wire taped green. Body, Arm, Dress—88 cm by 56 cm veleteen print, 100 cm of 1.5 cm lace. Shoes—36 cm by 16 cm navy blue velveteen, 14 cm by 10 cm purple felt. Also—pearl cotton, packing, cotton wadding, polyester batting.

(Doron): Head-Foundation, Arms, Legs—76 cm by 26 cm white rayon. Face, Nose, Arms—44 cm by 26 cm beige jersey. Legs—20 cm by 20 cm striped jersey. Eyes—dacron georgette. Mouth—strands of embroidery thread. Hair—

blue, gray worsted yarn. Body, Arms, Dress—90 cm by 43 cm blue gray velveteen, 26 cm of 1.5 cm braid, 22 cm of 2 cm braid, strands of embroidery cotton. Shoes—36 cm by 16 cm brown corduroy, 14 cm by 10 cm dark blue felt. Also—same as Rommy.

INSTRUCTIONS:

Make by referring to pages 50-64 for the basic method. Make nose from a scrap of cotton jersey colored in orange with felt-tip pen.

Body and arms are made of dress fabric.

Sew on marionette strings of pearl cotton cut in desired length.

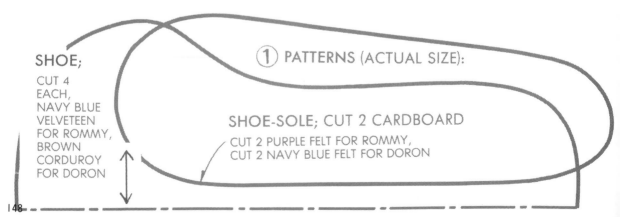

SHOE;

CUT 4 EACH, NAVY BLUE VELVETEEN FOR ROMMY, BROWN CORDUROY FOR DORON

① PATTERNS (ACTUAL SIZE):

SHOE-SOLE; CUT 2 CARDBOARD

CUT 2 PURPLE FELT FOR ROMMY,
CUT 2 NAVY BLUE FELT FOR DORON

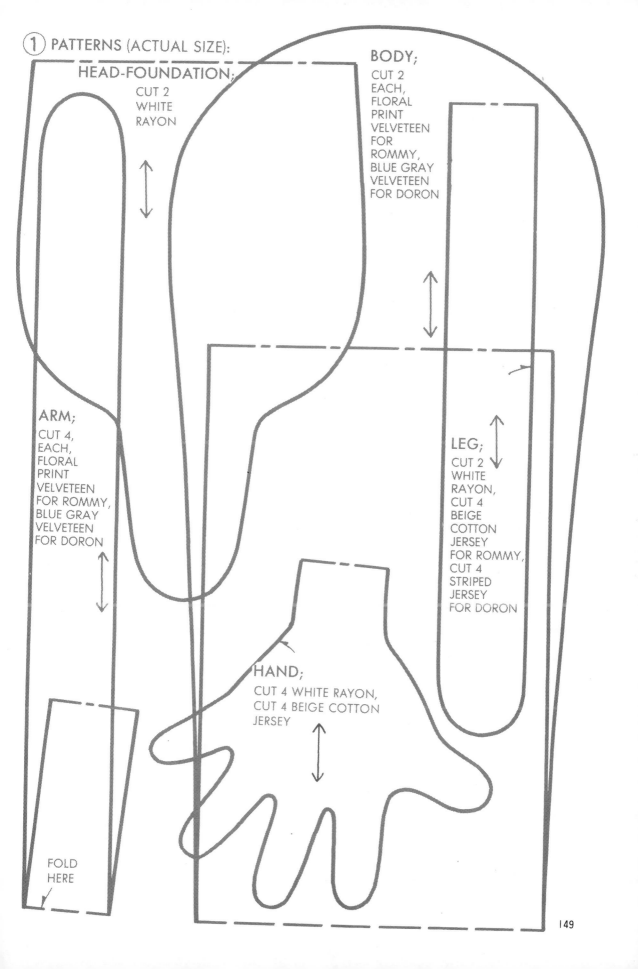

1 PATTERNS (ACTUAL SIZE):

HEAD-FOUNDATION;
CUT 2
WHITE
RAYON

BODY;
CUT 2
EACH,
FLORAL
PRINT
VELVETEEN
FOR
ROMMY,
BLUE GRAY
VELVETEEN
FOR DORON

ARM;
CUT 4,
EACH,
FLORAL
PRINT
VELVETEEN
FOR ROMMY,
BLUE GRAY
VELVETEEN
FOR DORON

LEG;
CUT 2
WHITE
RAYON,
CUT 4
BEIGE
COTTON
JERSEY
FOR ROMMY,
CUT 4
STRIPED
JERSEY
FOR DORON

HAND;
CUT 4 WHITE RAYON,
CUT 4 BEIGE COTTON
JERSEY

FOLD
HERE

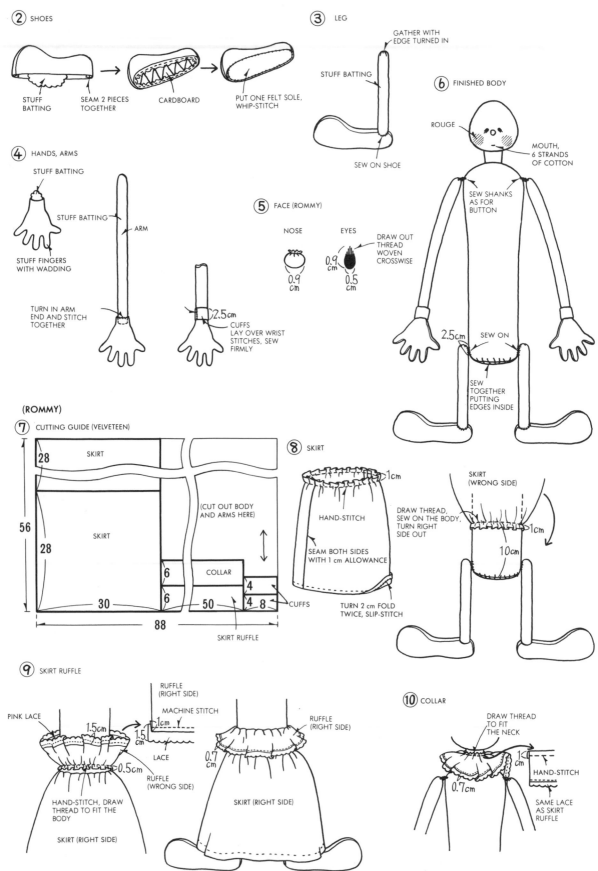

2 SHOES

STUFF BATTING — SEAM 2 PIECES TOGETHER — CARDBOARD — PUT ONE FELT SOLE, WHIP-STITCH

3 LEG

GATHER WITH EDGE TURNED IN

STUFF BATTING

SEW ON SHOE

4 HANDS, ARMS

STUFF BATTING

STUFF BATTING — ARM

STUFF FINGERS WITH WADDING

TURN IN ARM END AND STITCH TOGETHER

2.5cm

CUFFS LAY OVER WRIST STITCHES, SEW FIRMLY

5 FACE (ROMMY)

NOSE

0.9 cm

EYES

0.9 cm

DRAW OUT THREAD WOVEN CROSSWISE

0.5 cm

6 FINISHED BODY

ROUGE

MOUTH, 6 STRANDS OF COTTON

SEW SHANKS AS FOR BUTTON

2.5cm

SEW ON

SEW TOGETHER PUTTING EDGES INSIDE

(ROMMY)

7 CUTTING GUIDE (VELVETEEN)

28 — SKIRT

56

28 — SKIRT

30

88

6 / 6

COLLAR

50

(CUT OUT BODY AND ARMS HERE)

4 / 4 / 8

CUFFS

SKIRT RUFFLE

8 SKIRT

1cm

HAND-STITCH

SEAM BOTH SIDES WITH 1 cm ALLOWANCE

TURN 2 cm FOLD TWICE, SLIP-STITCH

SKIRT (WRONG SIDE)

DRAW THREAD, SEW ON THE BODY, TURN RIGHT SIDE OUT

1cm

10cm

9 SKIRT RUFFLE

PINK LACE

1.5cm

RUFFLE (RIGHT SIDE)

MACHINE STITCH

1cm

1.5 cm

LACE

0.5cm

RUFFLE (WRONG SIDE)

HAND-STITCH, DRAW THREAD TO FIT THE BODY

SKIRT (RIGHT SIDE)

RUFFLE (RIGHT SIDE)

0.7 cm

SKIRT (RIGHT SIDE)

10 COLLAR

DRAW THREAD TO FIT THE NECK

1 cm

HAND-STITCH

0.7cm

SAME LACE AS SKIRT RUFFLE

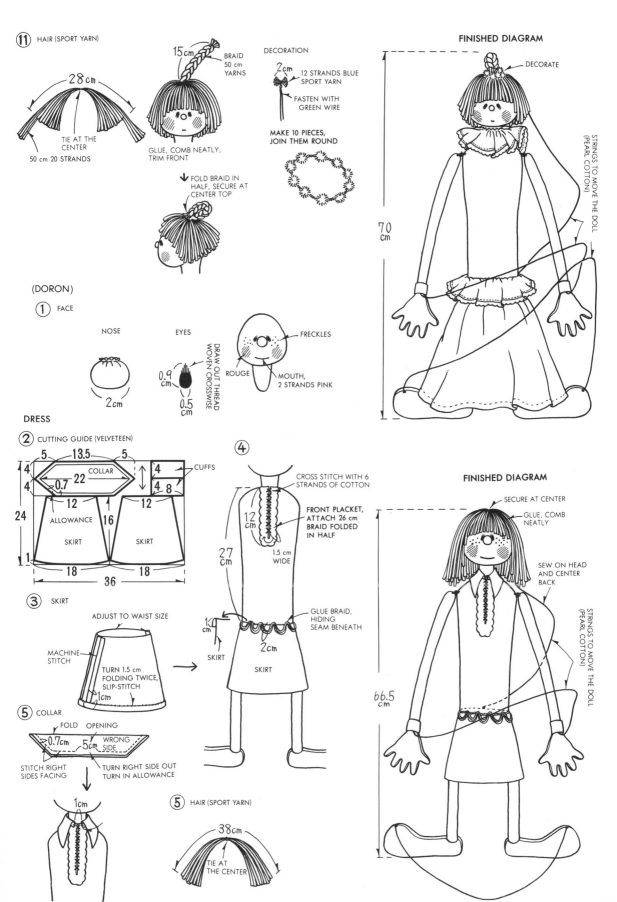

⑪ HAIR (SPORT YARN)

28 cm

TIE AT THE CENTER
50 cm 20 STRANDS

15cm

BRAID 50 cm YARNS

GLUE, COMB NEATLY, TRIM FRONT

↓ FOLD BRAID IN HALF, SECURE AT CENTER TOP

DECORATION

2 cm

12 STRANDS BLUE SPORT YARN

FASTEN WITH GREEN WIRE

MAKE 10 PIECES, JOIN THEM ROUND

FINISHED DIAGRAM

DECORATE

70 cm

STRINGS TO MOVE THE DOLL (PEARL COTTON)

(DORON)

① FACE

NOSE

2 cm

EYES

0.9 cm

0.5 cm

DRAW OUT THREAD WOVEN CROSSWISE

ROUGE

FRECKLES

MOUTH, 2 STRANDS PINK

DRESS

② CUTTING GUIDE (VELVETEEN)

5   13.5   5
4
COLLAR
4   0.7   22
4   8   CUFFS
12   12
24   ALLOWANCE   16
SKIRT   SKIRT
1
18   18
36

③ SKIRT

ADJUST TO WAIST SIZE

MACHINE STITCH

TURN 1.5 cm FOLDING TWICE, SLIP-STITCH

1cm

④

CROSS STITCH WITH 6 STRANDS OF COTTON

12 cm

FRONT PLACKET, ATTACH 26 cm BRAID FOLDED IN HALF

1.5 cm WIDE

27 cm

1 cm

SKIRT

GLUE BRAID, HIDING SEAM BENEATH

2cm

SKIRT

FINISHED DIAGRAM

SECURE AT CENTER

GLUE, COMB NEATLY

SEW ON HEAD AND CENTER BACK

66.5 cm

STRINGS TO MOVE THE DOLL (PEARL COTTON)

⑤ COLLAR

FOLD   OPENING

0.7cm   5cm   WRONG SIDE

STITCH RIGHT SIDES FACING

TURN RIGHT SIDE OUT TURN IN ALLOWANCE

1cm

⑤ HAIR (SPORT YARN)

38cm

TIE AT THE CENTER

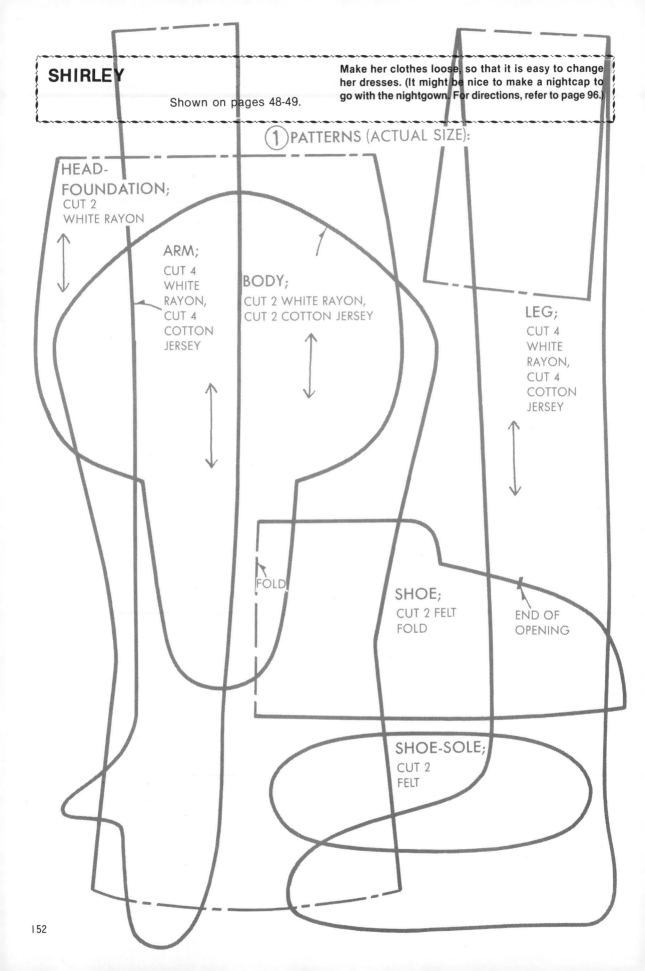

SHIRLEY

Shown on pages 48-49.

Make her clothes loose, so that it is easy to change her dresses. (It might be nice to make a nightcap to go with the nightgown. For directions, refer to page 96.)

① PATTERNS (ACTUAL SIZE):

HEAD-FOUNDATION;
CUT 2
WHITE RAYON

ARM;
CUT 4
WHITE
RAYON,
CUT 4
COTTON
JERSEY

BODY;
CUT 2 WHITE RAYON,
CUT 2 COTTON JERSEY

LEG;
CUT 4
WHITE
RAYON,
CUT 4
COTTON
JERSEY

FOLD

SHOE;
CUT 2 FELT
FOLD

END OF
OPENING

SHOE-SOLE;
CUT 2
FELT

YOU'LL NEED:

(Body): Head-Foundation, Body, Arms, Legs—90 cm by 56 cm white rayon. Face, Nose, Body, Arms, Legs—52 cm by 81 cm cotton jersey. Eyes—dacron georgette. Mouth—strands of embroidery thread. Hair—worsted-weight yarn.

(Underwear): 70 cm by 40 cm white broadcloth, 80 cm of 2 cm lace, 62 cm of 0.8 cm lace, 2 of 1 cm-diameter button, 10 cm of 0.5 cm elastic.

(Blouse): 90 cm by 37 cm crepe, 10 cm by 10 cm floral lace fabric, 3 of 1 cm-diameter button, 2 pair of small snaps.

(Jumper-skirt); 85 cm by 32 cm wool, 22 cm of 1.5 cm tyrolean tape, 20 cm long zipper fastener.

(Dress): 90 cm by 50 cm cotton print, 10 cm of 2 cm braid, 20 cm long zipper fastener.

(Skirt): 62 cm by 40 cm wool print, 40 cm of 0.5 cm elastic.

(Nightgown); 55 cm by 125 cm cotton border print, 17 cm of 1.3 cm lace, elastic thread, 20 cm long zipper fastener.

(Hat): Raffia yarn, 100 cm of 3.5 cm lace ribbon, artificial flower.

(Shoes): 21 cm by 15 cm felt, 40 cm of 0.3 cm ribbon.

FINISHED SIZE: 62 cm tall.

INSTRUCTIONS:

(Body): Make by referring to pages 50-64 for basic method. Sew on hair in same manner as for Karen on page 72. Finish allowances neatly, since seams are visible when clothes are changed.

(Underwear): Sew pants after the lace is sewn on. Fold back allowances of slip neck and armholes, insert lace and machine stitch.

(Blouse): Sew sleeve to side after sleeve top is joined. Sew lace fabric on front.

(Jumper-skirt): Make 7 pin tucks on front. Finish front neck with tyrolean tape.

(Dress): Finish front neck with its facing. Use selvage for hem ruffle. Pipe end of sleeve, sew underarm.

(Skirt): Make 2 rows of casing on the waist and pass elastic through.

(Nightgown): Make following border print pattern: Decorate front with shirring and finish with lace that is stitched on.

(Hat): Work single crochet firmly with size F hook. Finish with ribbon and flowers.

(Shoes): Join side piece and sole together, using silk thread; pass ribbon through, tie in position.

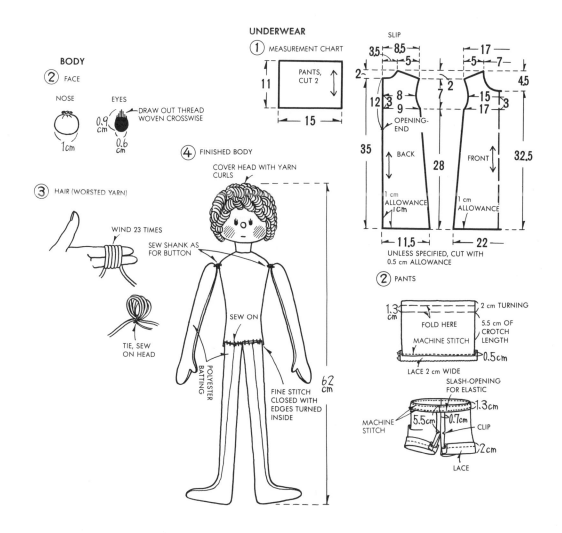

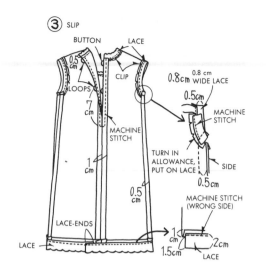

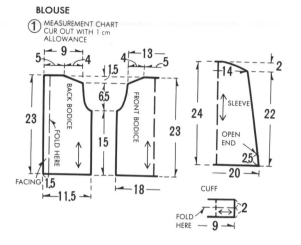

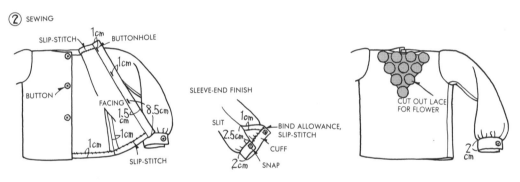

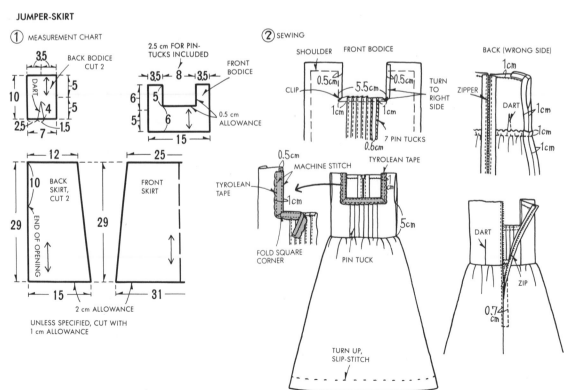

DRESS

① MEASUREMENT CHART

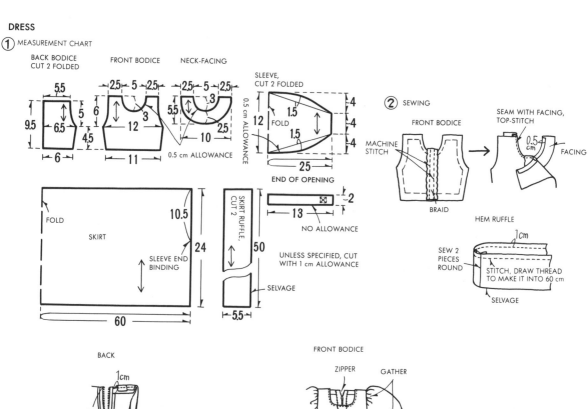

BACK BODICE
CUT 2 FOLDED

FRONT BODICE

NECK-FACING

5.5

9.5 | 6.5

6

5

4.5

2.5 — 5 — 2.5

6

12

3

11

0.5 cm ALLOWANCE

2.5 — 5 — 2.5

3

5.5

1

10

2.5

SLEEVE,
CUT 2 FOLDED

0.5 ALLOWANCE

12

FOLD

1.5

1.5

25

4

4

4

END OF OPENING

2

13

NO ALLOWANCE

UNLESS SPECIFIED, CUT
WITH 1 cm ALLOWANCE

② SEWING

FRONT BODICE

SEAM WITH FACING,
TOP-STITCH

MACHINE
STITCH

BRAID

0.5 cm

FACING

HEM RUFFLE

1cm

SEW 2
PIECES
ROUND

STITCH, DRAW THREAD
TO MAKE IT INTO 60 cm

SELVAGE

FOLD

SKIRT

10.5

24

SLEEVE END
BINDING

60

SKIRT RUFFLE,
CUT 2

50

SELVAGE

5.5

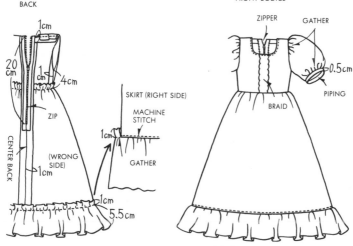

BACK

1cm

20 cm

1 cm

1cm

4cm

ZIP

CENTER BACK

(WRONG
SIDE)

1cm

SKIRT (RIGHT SIDE)

MACHINE
STITCH

1cm

GATHER

1cm

5.5 cm

FRONT BODICE

ZIPPER

GATHER

0.5cm

PIPING

BRAID

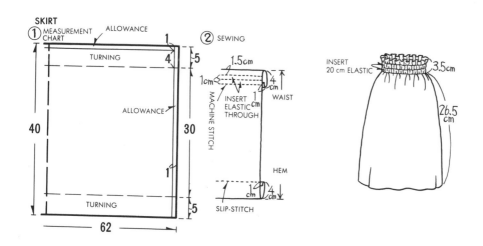

SKIRT

① MEASUREMENT
CHART

ALLOWANCE

TURNING

1

4

5

ALLOWANCE

40

30

1

1

TURNING

5

62

② SEWING

1.5cm

1cm

MACHINE STITCH

INSERT
ELASTIC
THROUGH

1cm

4

4

WAIST

HEM

1cm

4cm

SLIP-STITCH

INSERT
20 cm ELASTIC

3.5cm

26.5 cm

NIGHTGOWN

UNLESS SPECIFIED, CUT WITH 1 cm ALLOWANCE

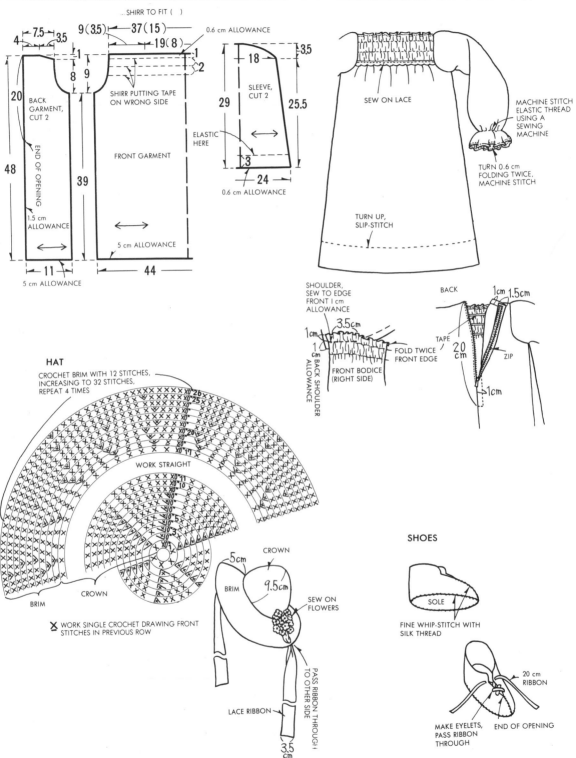

.. SHIRR TO FIT ( )

9(3.5) 37(15) 0.6 cm ALLOWANCE

4 7.5 3.5 19(8)

1 1

8 9 2

20 BACK GARMENT, CUT 2

END OF OPENING

48

1.5 cm ALLOWANCE

39

SHIRR PUTTING TAPE ON WRONG SIDE

FRONT GARMENT

ELASTIC HERE

5 cm ALLOWANCE

11 44

5 cm ALLOWANCE 5 cm ALLOWANCE

3.5 18

29 SLEEVE, CUT 2 25.5

3

24

0.6 cm ALLOWANCE

SEW ON LACE

MACHINE STITCH ELASTIC THREAD USING A SEWING MACHINE

TURN 0.6 cm FOLDING TWICE, MACHINE STITCH

TURN UP, SLIP-STITCH

SHOULDER, SEW TO EDGE FRONT 1 cm ALLOWANCE

BACK 1cm 1.5cm

3.5cm

1cm

1 cm BACK SHOULDER ALLOWANCE

FOLD TWICE FRONT EDGE

FRONT BODICE (RIGHT SIDE)

TAPE 20 cm ZIP

1cm

HAT

CROCHET BRIM WITH 12 STITCHES, INCREASING TO 32 STITCHES, REPEAT 4 TIMES

WORK STRAIGHT

BRIM CROWN

X WORK SINGLE CROCHET DRAWING FRONT STITCHES IN PREVIOUS ROW

5cm CROWN

BRIM 9.5cm

SEW ON FLOWERS

PASS RIBBON THROUGH TO OTHER SIDE

LACE RIBBON

3.5 cm

SHOES

SOLE

FINE WHIP-STITCH WITH SILK THREAD

20 cm RIBBON

MAKE EYELETS, PASS RIBBON THROUGH END OF OPENING